Ladies of Our Valley

By

Lucinda Ransick
Director, Santa Maria Valley Historical Society Museum

Edited by Michael W. Farris

JANAWAY PUBLISHING
Santa Maria, California

Copyright © 2020, SANTA MARIA VALLEY HISTORICAL SOCIETY

ALL RIGHTS RESERVED.
No part of this publication may be reproduced, stored in a
retrieval system, or transmitted in any form or by any
means whatsoever, whether electronic, mechanical,
magnetic recording, or photocopying, without the
prior written approval of the Copyright holder
or Publisher, excepting brief quotations
for inclusion in book reviews.

Author: Cindy Ransick

Editor: Michael W. Farris

Published for Santa Maria Valley Historical Society

by:

Janaway Publishing, Inc.
732 Kelsey Ct.
Santa Maria, California 93454
(805) 925-1038
www.janawaygenealogy.com

2020

Library of Congress Control Number: 2020944853

ISBN: 978-1-59641-455-6

Copies of this book may be purchased from Santa Maria Valley Historical Society, 616 S. Broadway, Santa Maria, CA 93454.
For more information, please write, or phone (805) 922-3130.

Made in the United States of America

Dedicated to JoAnn McBride

The ladies in this book were each painstakingly selected by JoAnn McBride. Without her, this first volume of ladies would still be in an old mauve colored, metal filing cabinet. Thank you, JoAnn, for your excellent organizing skills, keen eye and wonderful sense of humor.

JoAnn Walker McBride, was born in Ada, Oklahoma, on February 1, 1930. She had one sister. She graduated from East Central University in Ada with a B.S. in Business Administration and a M.S. in Education.

JoAnn married Ray Peak, whom she met at college and had two children: DiAnn and Joe.

JoAnn was an elementary school teacher in Oklahoma for two years and then, when her family relocated to Santa Maria in 1959, worked for Fairlawn Elementary School for over 20 years. She was offered a position as a Program Specialist with the Santa Barbara County

Pictures provided by JoAnne's daughter DiAnne Ferguson.

Public School District Office and worked in that capacity for 10 years, until she retired in 1985.

Not being a person to sit around, she forged a new career after retirement and was involved in several voluntary capacities, such as a Board Member for SMILE (Santa Maria Independent Living Environment) for a number of years before joining the Board of Directors at the Santa Maria Valley Historical Society. JoAnn's tireless work with the Historical Society served to uncover several pieces of valuable history associated with the Santa Maria Valley.

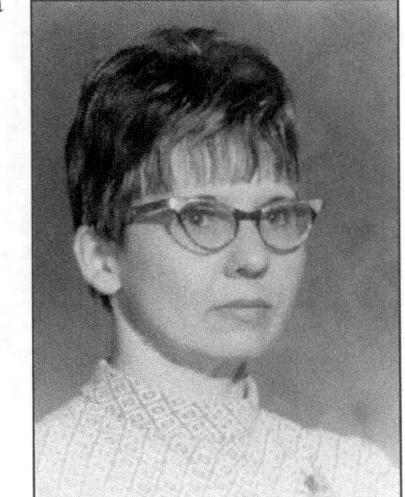

Table of Contents

Ladies of Our Valley

Dedicated to JoAnn McBride iii

Ladies of Our Valley 1

Introduction 3

Chapter One: First Ladies of Our Valley 7
    Eduarda Osuna Foxen (1812-1894) 8
    Nancy Roberts Kelsey (1823-1896) 11
    Ramona Foxen Wickenden (1839-1919) 13

Chapter Two: Santa Maria Pioneers 15
    Elizabeth Conner Adam (1839-1898) 16
    Elizabeth Booth Bradley (1840-1903) 18
    Abigail Trott Bryant Wiley (1840-1924) 20
    Mary Long Rice (1836-1936) 22
    Harriett Sharp Hart (1844-1896) 24
    Anna Van Valkenburg Blosser (1846-1926) 27
    Margaret McHenry Tietzen (1859-1946) 29
    Anastasia Adam Porter (1871-1954) 31

Chapter Three: The Four Ladies of the Four Corners 33
    Minerva Marshall Maulsby Thornburgh (1820-1898) 35
    Mary Nancy Barnes Fesler (1822-1895) 38
    Anna Robrecht Miller (1838-1917) 40
    Janetti Lillian Nelson Cook (1838-1896) 42

Chapter Four: Town Builders 45
    Mary Olive Earl Winters (1861-1946) 46
    Henrietta Louise Newlove Martin (1870-1921) 48
    Mary Antoinette McClain Blosser (1865-1958) 50
    Eleonore Begou Renoult Roemer (1865-1939) 52

Table of Contents

Sarah Jane Dayment Smith (1844-1938) 54

Elizabeth Mary Oakley May (1895-1981) 56

Chapter Five: Splitting Centuries 59

Sarah Frances Harris Lewis (1858-1951) 60

Minna "Minnie" Allott Stearns (1863-1948) 62

Ida May Twitchell Blochman (1854-1931) 64

Lucretia Hazel Reynolds Smith (1875-1936) 68

Virginia Grossini Barca Ziliotto (1884-1949) 71

Ethel Elma Pope (1885-1969) 73

Mary Lola Paulding (1887-1976) 75

Angelina Linda Pertusi Ontiveros (1894-1998) 78

Odulia Anna Carranza Dille (1897-1990) 81

Chapter Six: Coming of Age in a New Century 84

Ethel May Palmer Dorsey Conrad (1902-1991) 85

Olga Pauline Giacomini Weldon (1903-2006) 89

Thelma Louise Chamberlain Battles (1906-2008) 91

Laura Jane Stair Smith Harris (1914-1982) 93

Patricia Jean Boyd (1920-2012) 96

Chapter Seven: Charitable Societies 98

Minerva Club 98

Improvement Club 99

TBDL Club 100

A to Z Club 101

Chapter Eight: The Stories They Tell 102

Dedications 103

Ladies of Our Valley

Elizabeth Adam	Henrietta Martin
Virginia Barca	Elizabeth May
Thelma Battles	Anna Miller
Ida Blochman	Erlinda Ontiveros
Anna Blosser	Mary Paulding
Mary Blosser	Ethel Pope
Patricia Boyd	Anastasia Porter
Elizabeth Bradley	Mary Rice
Janetti Cook	Eleonore Roemer
Odulia Dille	Lucretia Smith
Ethel May Dorsey	Sarah Jane Smith
Nancy Fesler	Minnie Stearns
Eduarda Foxen	Minerva Thornburgh
Jane Harris	Olga Weldon
Harriet Hart	Ramona Wickenden
Nancy Kelsey	Abigail Wiley
Sarah Lewis	Mary Winters

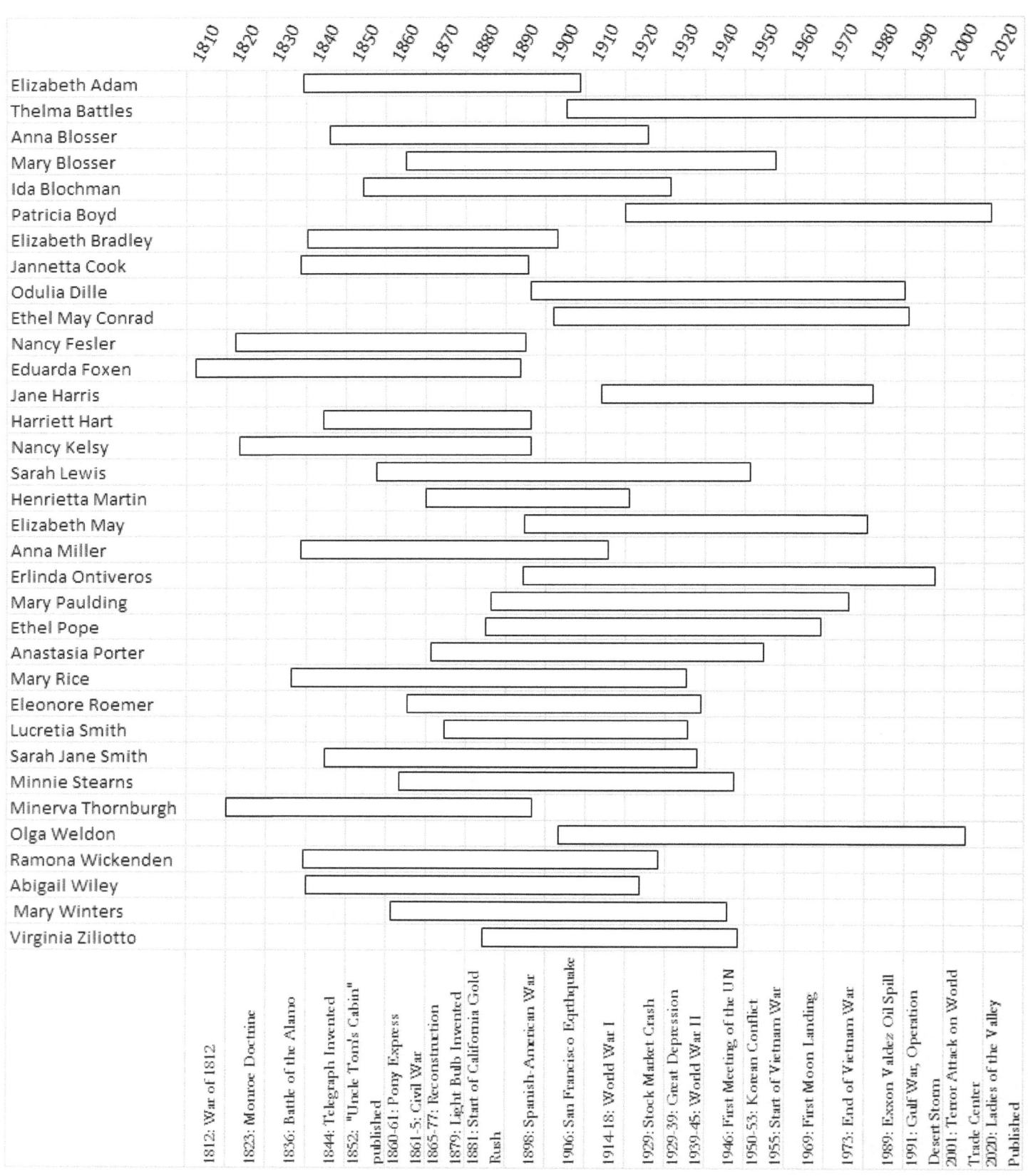

Introduction

A lot is owed to the trailblazing, adventurous, frontier women of the late nineteenth century. Arriving from countries both near and far, of all ages, with little to nothing or sometimes towing a piano and with a child on her hip and another by the hand, the frontier woman cleared a pathway to the west. Today, the twenty-first century woman is in almost every conceivable place and profession because her frontier predecessor stepped out of the confines of her kitchen; sometimes barefoot and laced in a corset.

The Central Coast of California can proudly boast of the vigor, endured hardship and utter determination of its women. As the population of the Santa Maria Valley grew, it clearly benefitted from the presence of these intrepid womenfolk. The Victorians had held the mistaken belief that a woman was frail, vulnerable and in need of protection. Her mind was held to be weaker than any man's and should be kept free of complicated thoughts such as mathematics and politics, but it was the destiny of the delicate female to transform much of the western United States.

Our own valley was flush with the pioneering spirit that transformed dusty, blustery, and seemingly barren spaces into the prosperous, beautiful Central Coast it is today. These westering women imposed standards of living that men had grown unaccustomed to after years of roaming the backwaters and the wilds of open land. The ladies were not down for bypassing all the comforts and conveniences over a sheer lack of concern for what might be called the "niceties." They were very persuasive to those frontier men who wanted to become husbands and fathers. If a man was willing to take a wife, it meant he was prepared to build her a home, a town, a school; in short, a decent life.

Nancy Kelsey, the epitome of the frontier woman.
Model by artist-historian George Stuart.

Even as their forefathers before them had learned in Jamestown, and corrected in Plymouth, successful homesteading could best be done when it included women. One of the first clues the Wampanoag Indians had at Plymouth that the English were going to stay, and not just plunder the land and leave, was that women had accompanied the men. Exploring had largely been man's work in the New World. Indigenous people across the continent had tolerated intrusions and plundering to a great extent as they watched with certainty the men come and go from the land. It did not go unnoticed when families began arriving. It was the men who came with wives and daughters who would change the world forever. These pilgrims built their houses firmly attached to the ground.

Introduction

Destination Golden West

The colonization of California began with the Spanish Empire's discovery of New Spain. At its pinnacle, New Spain included what are today Mexico, Central America to the Isthmus of Panama, Florida, and much of the West Indies, as well as the Philippines and the southwestern United States which included the states of Texas, Arizona, New Mexico, and California.

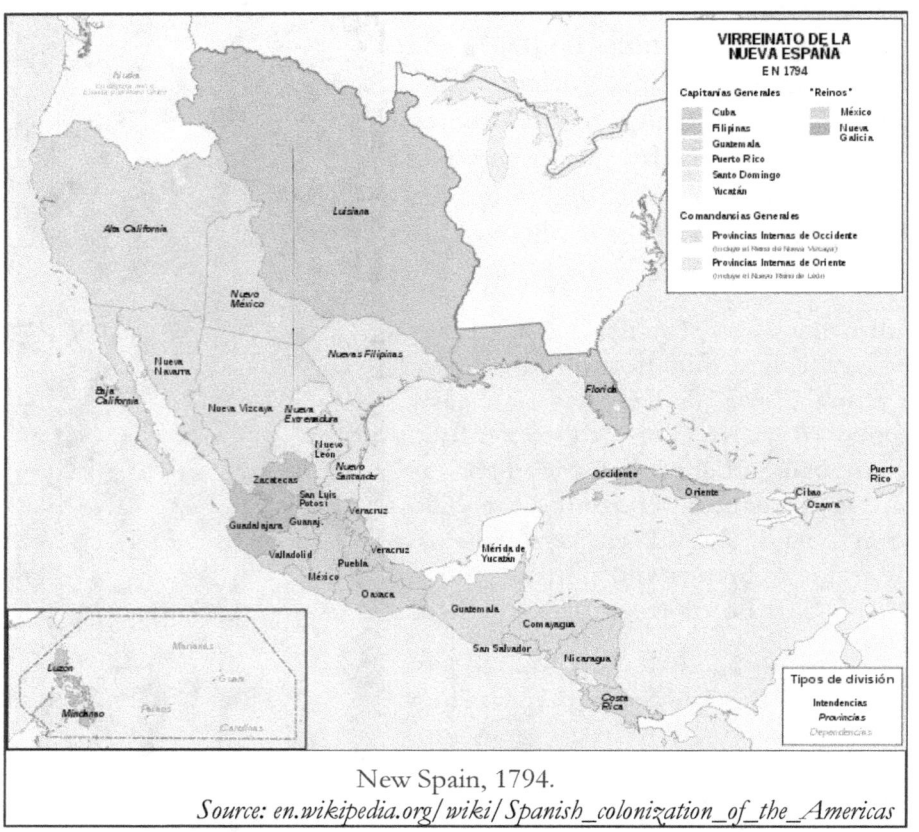

New Spain, 1794.
Source: en.wikipedia.org/wiki/Spanish_colonization_of_the_Americas

The romantic pastoral days of California's history began with Spain granting Mexico independence. Agustin de Iturbide defeated the royalist forces opposed to the independence of Mexico, and the new Spanish viceroy, Juan de O'Donojú, lacking money, provisions, and troops, was forced to accept independence. On August 24, 1821, O'Donojú signed the Treaty of Córdoba, thus ending much of New Spain's dependence on Old Spain.

The new Mexican government encouraged settlement of the coastal region of Alta California by giving prominent men large land grants called ranchos, usually two or more square leagues, or 14 square miles. Land-grant titles were government-issued, permanent, unencumbered property-ownership rights to land. The ranchos encompassed virtually all of the most valuable land. Given to raising cattle and sheep, the owners of the ranchos patterned themselves after the landed gentry of Spain. Mexico granted about 270 ranchos between 1833 and 1846.

The size of these land grants made homes isolated, so they needed to be able to support the family. There were no towns or stores close by. Travel was arduous, by horseback or *carreta*. Any travel to visit other family or friends was a laborious experience that took time and, as such, was done rarely as the land could not spare the family the time needed to come and go and still care for animals and crops; most traveled only a few miles from their homes in their lifetime. It would have been a lonely existence for a man alone. It was an isolating experience for a woman whose man left at sunrise to work the land and returned for dinner. Children certainly added to life, but the yearning for the company of other women created a determination within these frontier wives that would lead to the development of towns and communities.

Introduction

In the years after the Civil War, women found plenty of opportunities in the West that were not available in the East: everything from the right to vote, equal pay, and more liberal divorce laws. The West was the first home of women's suffrage in the United States, with nearly every western state and territory enfranchising women long before ladies won the right to vote in any eastern state.

Clipart courtesy of Florida Center for Instructional Technology: etc.usf.edu/clipart

The enticement of mining had opened California to migration, and mostly men made the initial trek westward hoping to make a fortune but spend it back east on their wives or girlfriends. As the twinkle of gold and the flash of silver faded, many other attributes and opportunities in the West became evident, and the peregrinations of bachelorhood, with men bounding from scheme-to-scheme and camp-to-camp, ended. The advancing realization was that if a man was going to stay out west, life was better with a woman!

By 1857, women represented 50 percent of the emigrants in the wagon trains. Women found it within themselves to traverse the country in covered wagons, children striding alongside. Other women had to brave the sea in all manner of floating vessels traveling through the Straits of Magellan to come west. Whether arriving by land or sea, the male-female ratio decreased from a staggering 12:1 to 2:1 over the course of a decade. The message was clearly understood. Women were smart, strong, talented and made the uncertainties of life more bearable. They gave their men purpose, direction, and, above all, standards.

In 1869 Isaac Miller, Rudolph Cook, and Isaac Fesler arrived in the Santa Maria Valley. Then, in 1871, John Thornburgh cast his shadow in the valley. Much is made of our town fathers. These new rural Californians shared many burdens, socialized together, bartered goods. Eventually communities were established around their farms and ranches. Mrs. Miller, Mrs. Cook, Mrs. Fesler and Mrs. Thornburgh, their first names virtually unspoken, would shape a town.

Most early Santa Maria Valley men arrived in the valley with wives and families in tow. The ladies of the valley arrived at all ages and stages of life, and with varied pasts, knowing what they wanted and

Introduction

needed. They wanted other female neighbors, plentiful and good quality foods, education for their children, churches to worship in and culture to grow their families around. The valley men readily accepted these terms. Keeping wives and the young women who had arrived in the West happy attracted more women, and this made young working men happy and more productive! The single men and husbands built houses and schools; purchased dairy cows, sheep and poultry; dug wells; and started vegetable gardens in order to have households based on the family. Those early days of dwelling in dugouts, lean-tos and bathing irregularly had given way to the desires, demands and needs of these brave westering women.

Hart home, 1892
Source: Santa Maria Valley Historical Society collection.

Land seemed vast and populations small in those first years. Land grants, ranchos, haciendas, farms, whatever the configuration, there was available arable land with room to breathe, build families and enjoy the fruits of prosperity. The ladies overcame the hardships of hauling water, bearing children, and living isolated with a frontier man. They were transforming the nation; building a nation for the world to admire.

In our valley in 1894, though spread widely apart and living modestly, twenty-five women gathered with the intention of advancing their position in life for their children, boys and girls alike. They were originally known as the Ladies Literary Society and later as the Minerva Club. They would be responsible for the first park, the first picnic, and the first library.

Even as our town came to take shape late in the nineteenth century under the nurture of the ladies of the Ladies Literary Society, there were a few brave women who lived and died before them. They provided the foundation of a community for those gals who came next.

Chapter One: First Ladies of Our Valley

Young girls who reached womanhood in the period from 1621 to the 1800s were generally raised to hope and pray for a good husband. A good husband was, by definition, one who would treat her as well as he treated his cattle or his horse. Young brides were 13-14 years old, barely women at all. Strong physically, they proved capable of enduring many hardships. These girls, many extremely naïve as they entered marriage, faced harsh realities, usually with much older husbands. Cooking over hot fires, bearing a child nearly every year, they were indoctrinated to the idea that pleasing their husbands was their purpose as they lived very isolated lives. Many ladies were destined to exceed expectations as they moved from a subsistence life style to become a new breed of frontier woman with a mind, will and destiny of her own making. Although there were many young brides, it is a misconception that most girls married in their teens. While marriage was often expected and satisfied many basic needs, mostly financial, women born during the Elizabethan and Jacobean eras married much later than many people realize. Data taken from birthdates of women and marriage certificate between the years 1566-1837 reveals mean marriage ages to have been 25-27 years.

Isaac Miller, Jr., and bride Edith Miller wedding picture, c. 1895
Source: Santa Maria Valley Historical Society collection.

The age of consent was 12 for a girl, 14 for a boy, but for most children puberty came two or three years later than it does today.

The reason for late marriage among the middleclass was simple enough: it took a long time for a couple to acquire enough belongings to set up housekeeping, even in a room of their parents' home. Young love, however romantic, had to be kept in check if the two lovers were to survive in a world where subsistence earnings could not purchase a roof over their heads and put food on the table. Children of noble birth ran a great risk if they tried to marry without the approval of their parents, since they would be left without resources. The average marital age of women was closer to 25 in this period.

High mortality rates among both men and women often led to "convenience" marriages that gave a bereaved husband a wife to help with his young children and a young widow a husband willing and able to support her and the children of her previous marriage. These blended families soon welcomed even more children fulfilling the yours, mine and ours of family growth. Marriage was as much business as it was pleasure in the rough and tumble expansion regions of our nation.

Chapter One: First Ladies of Our Valley

Eduarda Osuna Foxen (1812-1894)

Eduarda Osuna Foxen
Donated to the Santa Maria Valley Historical Society by Winston Wickenden.

Eduarda Foxen and her twin sister Antonia Maria were born October 13, 1812, to Jose Maria del Carmen Osuna and Maria Antonia Cota. Raised in Santa Barbara, Eduarda was 19 years old when she met William Benjamin Foxen at the home of her step-father, Tomas Antonio Olivera.

Foxen, an English sea captain, was in his mid-thirties when he caught his first glance at the slender dark-eyed Eduarda. In her home on business with Olivera, Foxen was totally smitten after only catching a glimpse of her. In short order, Foxen would sell his boat and cargo. He reorganized his assets and established a general merchandise store, building comfortable living quarters overhead so that he could be close the girl who had stolen his heart. They had barely met, yet he knew in his heart he wanted to marry her. No words had even passed between them as she spoke no English and he spoke no Spanish.

Foxen approached Don Olivera for Eduarda's hand. Foxen was informed that the girls in the family were not permitted to marry outside of the Catholic Church; if he wanted Eduarda, he had to become a Catholic. Foxen agreed; after all, this was little to ask from a man who had abandoned the sea, became a merchant and built an apartment just for the chance to court the lovely Eduarda! Olivera brokered the marriage proposal assuring his step-daughter that Foxen was a "good man."

Foxen might have been a good man, but Eduarda had a prominent bloodline. She was the daughter of Jose Maria del Carmen Osuna, one of three brothers who came first to Mexico from Spain, then to Alta California. It was claimed they were related to the Counts of Osuna, nobles of Alhambra of Spain. Eduarda's mother was the daughter of Pablo Cota who was born in Spain and came to California with Father Junipero Serra. Cota was a direct descendent of the ancient Galician family of Lugo for which the province of Lugo in Spain is named.

Don Olivera may have considered it a favorable match, but he very much wanted the Englishman Foxen to understand he was marrying up by their family estimations, and he expected Foxen to prove himself a worthy partner.

After their wedding, Eduarda lived by a new standard, luxuriously with her husband in the home he had designed above his store. She, who had always been accustomed to an adobe, must have found it a wonderful new home. The floors were not earthen but board with beautiful rag rugs. She had an enviable view of the ocean and the city's streets and her husband was within calling distance in the store below. Eduarda's marriage was proving a most happy one and soon the babies started arriving. Their life was comfortable and prosperous.

Chapter One: First Ladies of Our Valley

Eventually, the Foxens became restless in the confines of town and, with a growing family, the idea of more space spurred them to purchase Rancho Tinaquaic in 1837 from Victor Linares. After undertaking the arduous task of building an adobe, Foxen moved Eduarda and their three children from the safety of town to an underdeveloped location without roads or even trouble-free access. Their rancho was 75 miles distant from her life in Santa Barbara. Dona Eduarda's life on the rancho was very busy. She was serious minded, extremely neat, and held herself with great baring. In her household she had Indian servants, but they were untrained. All clothes were made and sewn by hand. It was said that she made clothes from the sail of her husband's former ship. She made several varieties of cheese by using rennet made from the stomach of a calf. Candles were also hand made using tallow and beeswax. Most household chores were made difficult by a lack of convenience to water and the need for heat, which was generated by open fire in hearths or wood burning stoves. Her days of scrunching her toes in rag rugs and peering out to the ocean while enjoying the fresh breeze had transitioned to motherhood and the busy schedule of a frontier lifestyle.

There were many tribes of Indians around the rancho, and Eduarda would give food, water, or comfort to any that approached in need. She was courageous and tactful in her dealings as she was often alone with her children when the men worked riding the range and tending the cattle. It happened that one day while sewing and watching her children that a band of naked Indians approached. Boisterous and appearing treacherous, they approached her cautiously at first. According to Eduarda, she was putting the finishing stitches in a red flannel petticoat that she had been laboring over for days. Red, a provocative color, incited great enthusiasm in the Indians, and they rushed to her knee for a closer look. Thinking quickly, Eduarda took up her scissors, cut her prized possession into portions for each of the Indians. They decorated themselves and with shouts of joy danced about before leaving the family and homestead untouched.

In danger from animals, danger from Indians, and danger from sickness or injury, the ladies of the frontier had to be prepared. Remedies, recipes, and general homemaking skills were handed down from mother to daughter. Eduarda was well prepared to be a frontier wife and understood the medicinal value of herbs. Adjacent to the Foxen home was a spot called "the drug store"; medicinal herbs of great variety abounded there. Eduarda was responsible for therapies, cures and tonics for anything that ailed her family, neighbors or even the local Indians. Eduarda's life was demanding and her days long.

"For the Good of the Country," by Hattie Benefield Stone, contains an extensive description of Eduarda's life. *The book is available for review in the Santa Maria Valley Historical Society research library.*

Eduarda reportedly gave birth eighteen times of which eleven grew up. Truly we know very little about her joys and sadness. We understand that her life was very fulfilled from the stories that have filtered down through generations of her descendants.

The obituary of Mrs. Eduarda Foxen concludes: "As the clock was striking the hour of six, surrounded by her weeping children, relatives and friends, and before the last echo of the clock died away, the life spark of a kind mother, a true friend and a Christian-spirited lady crossed the dark river at the age of eighty-two years, five months and nineteen days."

The Foxen Adobe Remains
Source: Santa Maria Valley Historical Society collection.

Nancy Roberts Kelsey (1823-1896)

Nancy Kelsy
Source: Santa Maria Valley Historical Society collection.

There is almost as much myth and mystery to the life of Nancy Kelsey as there are cold hard facts. In an interview with Kelsey published in the *San Francisco Examiner*, where she recollected the trip across the continent, she said the group had "no guide and no compass," but Nancy had a destiny that is both charted and reminisced.

She was born Nancy Roberts, August 1, 1823, in Barren County, Kentucky. Nancy's family was not known for being well polished or very educated. The Kelseys were also reputed to be rough and tough, barely able to read and write, uneducated by even the most modest standards. Nancy once remarked that she could remember things so well because her mind wasn't stuffed so full of education as minds are at her age. Together from an early age, Nancy and Ben Kelsey were married when Nancy was only 15 years old. They scratched out a living on their own, hunting and trading for dry goods.

Ben refused to settle down in one place, whether prosperous or starving. Throughout their lives together, that would never change. Ben Kelsey was constantly relocating into uncivilized and poorly chartered territories, Nancy always at his side. No matter the many dangers and hardships encountered in the untamed West, Nancy followed him, babes in her arms.

Nancy Kelsey was the first white woman to travel overland from Missouri, seeing Utah (also the first white woman to see the Great Salt Lake) and Nevada before crossing the Sierra Nevada mountains into California on November 25, 1841. She was a member of the Bartleson-Bidwell party. The 1841 Bartleson-Bidwell Party was the first group of emigrants to travel overland to California along the route that would become known as the California Trail. Numbering more than sixty, the group had formed somewhat spontaneously as wagons gathered and provisions were bought at a "jumping off point." It was decided that it would be safer to travel in larger numbers to California. The group would eventually splinter with parts heading to Oregon.

It was during their time in Sonoma that Nancy donated cloth for, and helped stitch, the first bear flag. Later she and another woman supposedly sewed shirts for pathfinder, explorer and soldier John Fremont and his troops. The mother of eight surviving children, she is sometimes referred to as the "Betsy Ross of California" for her role in the creation of the original Bear Flag from which the Bear Flag Rebellion got its name.

> The way to California was not of government development but an unimproved pathway worn in by a few men emigrating in 1840. The efforts of three parties had established a passable wagon road over the two main obstacles west: the Great Salt Lake Desert in Utah and the Sierra Nevada Mountains in California. The journey of 2,008 miles was undertaken in a single summer and fall, most traveling by oxen, horse or mule at a pace of about 15 miles a day. This meant an expedition of about five months.

Chapter One: First Ladies of Our Valley

Over the years, she endured many frightening encounters with Indians: killings, the scalping of one of her daughters, and the loss of all of their money made from gold field diggings, to name only a few major confrontations. The nomadic Kelseys can be tracked through many frontier places: on a cattle drive along the northern coast, a trading post on the Sacramento River, a flour mill near Sonoma, a toll ferry on the Kern River and a log cabin in Napa Valley. In 1859, the Kelseys and their two daughters were in Mexico before moving on to Texas where they were attacked by Comanche Indians. They continued to journey from territory-to-territory and state-to-state until Ben's death in 1889 in Los Angeles.

The original Bear Flag, designed by William L. Todd, sewn by Nancy Kelsey, Mrs. John Sears and Mrs. Benjamin Dewell. It was lost to fire in the 1906 San Francisco earthquake.
https://en.wikipedia.org/wiki/Nancy_Kelsey

Nancy, now a widow, decided to abandon life in the bustle of Los Angeles and returned to nature. It is unclear why she chose Cottonwood Canyon, but it seems likely because Martha Ann, the baby she carried across the Sierras, had married a man in Cuyama, a dozen miles east.

Nancy was very knowledgeable in the use of medicinal herbs. She was a familiar figure on her pinto pony, riding over the sparsely settled valley ministering to the ailing and helping bring new babies into the world.

Her life without Ben, settled in the valley, was a busy one. However, something was very wrong with Nancy. There were two Santa Marians who became especially interest in Nancy's desperate situation, Ida Blochman and Addison Powell. Nancy was living a meager existence. When she began to feel poorly, it was Ida Blochman who arranged for her to be brought to town in a spring wagon and examined in Santa Maria by Drs. William T. Lucas and H.C. Bagby. They found an inoperable cancer, and she was returned to her chicken farm to await her end.

Her life adventures were the stuff of history. Although she is all but forgotten, she was the first pioneer woman to cross the western desert and climb the Sierras into California. She did most of it barefooted and with her oldest daughter in her arms. She lived in a flimsy cabin and died an impoverished widow, August 10, 1896, in Cuyama, California. She lies in a remote grave deep in the mountains east of Santa Maria alongside the creek in Cottonwood Canyon. Nancy made a final request to be buried in a "store coffin." Through the generosity of the Santa Maria community, the purchase was made, and the coffin was kept protected and undercover at her undeclared homestead until she was ready to take up residence. Her remote and humble last resting place is all the more remarkable because of her courageous and adventurous life.

Nancy Kelsey's pioneering life was recognized in 1950 by the Native Daughters of the Golden West, Santa Maria Parlor. Three other counties joined the Santa Maria Parlor in honoring her memory by establishing a highway monument on public land. Erected near her final resting place on private property it commemorates her life of hardship, adventure and bravery as she traversed the then unknown West.

Ramona Foxen Wickenden (1839-1919)

Ramona Foxen Wickenden
Source: Santa Maria Valley Historical Society collection.

Ramona was the eldest daughter of William Benjamin and Eduarda Osuna Foxen. The Foxen sisters, Eduarda's daughters, often road 50 miles on horseback to visit relatives, attend church and, if the opportunity presented, to fandango, or dance. It was during one of these outings that Ramona met a handsome Englishman, Frederick Wickenden. Much as her mother before her, she made a love-match with a "foreigner." Similar to his soon-to-be father-in-law, Wickenden had been quickly smitten. He took every opportunity to visit Ramona at Rancho Tinaquaic and, before many months, they were wed. Unlike Foxen, Wickenden was Spanish speaking.

It was a time when the prescription for a "good marriage" was determined by the simple requirement of managing the basics: if a young woman could serve a good meal, tend the sick, sew a straight seam, ride a horse, and was somewhat musical in voice or instrument, she was an excellent prospect! Ramona Foxen was much more than expected. Ramona was considered quite accomplished in all of those things and many more. While many marriages were created based on need, practicality or even barter, Ramona and Frederick had love, an unexpected bonus in their time and, considering the hardships of pioneer life, a great blessing.

In 1862, the bride and groom built their home in Foxen Canyon. Ramona's father gave them a large tract of land for their own use on Rancho Tinaquaic. They decided on sheep ranching. Their new home was a small adobe, but the following winter it rained for forty days and nights. The walls of the house collapsed. They could not flee to the Foxen home because the creek swelled above flood level and blocked their escape. Wickenden took a long table, put up poles over it and stretched sheets and blankets to make a tent.

The Wickendens had many financial ups and downs due to draught, flood, and other unpredictable natural adversities. Ramona's inheritance was definitely one of the ups despite the many challenges! Her share of Rancho Tinaquaic was near the mouth of Foxen Canyon. A stage company organized a line running from San Francisco to Los Angeles by way of Gaviota Pass. Taking advantage of their proximity, they opened a store and stage stop, accepting the mail. Their home/business became quite the gathering place for families, and it was eventually designated a stagecoach station.

The Wickendens had a lot of contact with travelers from the north and south. Since the rancho was centrally located, businessmen met to discuss matters of local and national interest. The stages brought all manner of folks through the rancho. The speed at which the stagecoaches travelled was a modern marvel! Horses, six to eight-in-hand traveling at a gallop, reached nearly 8 miles per hour. Besides business men, there were miners with tales of the Sierras. The stage drivers themselves were a jovial lot. Life on Rancho Tinaquaic had taken on a whole new *persona*; being no longer an isolated hard-to-reach destination made life more of an adventure and less of a hardship.

Chapter One: First Ladies of Our Valley

In 1872, additional acreage was purchased from the government by the Wickendens. The whole community (the ladies especially) desired a convenient place where church services could be held and children (Ramona had eight) could receive proper catechism instructions without the long journey to Mission Santa Ynez, the closest church. Additionally, Ramona wanted a proper resting place for her beloved father, William Benjamin Foxen, and a cemetery at the chapel would serve nicely. Wickenden took 5,000 sheep north in 1875, a draught year, and found water and grass, eventually selling his stock for $1 each. The profit was used to purchase and ship redwood boards back to Tinaquaic, enough to add eight rooms to the adobe and to build a church. Completed in 1875 and consecrated as the Chapel San Ramon, Frederick Wickenden, Thomas Foxen and Chris Lawson, a carpenter from Los Alamos, are thought to have done most of the work. A husband's desire to please his beloved wife created the first historical landmark in Santa Barbara County.

SAN RAMON CHAPEL | 1875

Source: santamariavalley.com

On January 18, 1915, Ramona School was organized by petition, named for Ramona Oil Company, which was named for Ramona Foxen Wickenden. On Monday, October 1, 1919, with little fanfare, Ramona Foxen Wickenden was laid to rest at Calvary Cemetery, not the graveyard of the little chapel she inspired. Her husband preceded her in death in January of the same year at the age of 92.

Chapter Two: Santa Maria Pioneers

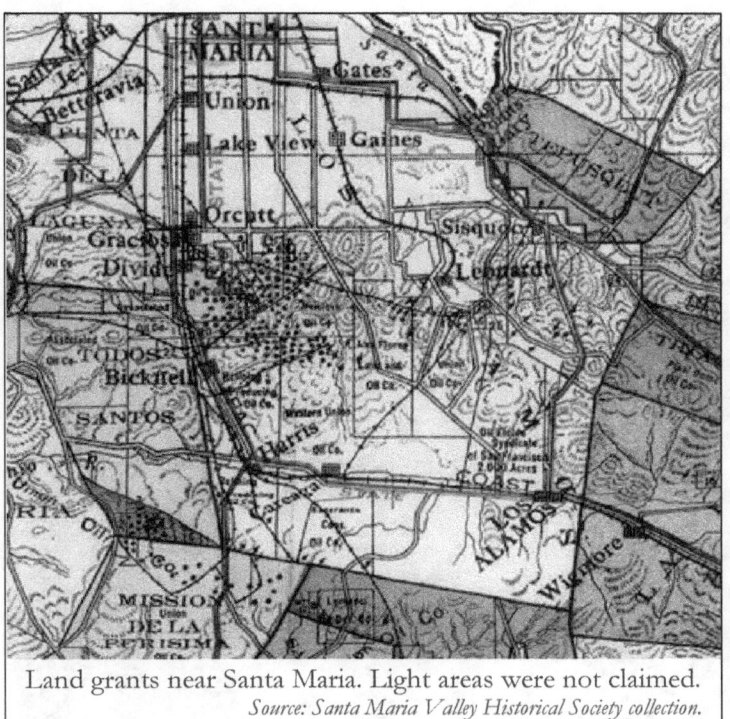
Land grants near Santa Maria. Light areas were not claimed.
Source: Santa Maria Valley Historical Society collection.

Leading the land-seekers in our valley was a courageous, kindly, widowed, farmer named Benjamin T. Wiley. In 1867, he became the first settler on unclaimed land that lay between Spanish ranchos of the Santa Maria Valley. Despite its sparse apparent attributes, he liked what he saw and staked his claim. Others must have agreed that the valley held promise because a trickle of excited families followed in quick procession: John Prell, George Washington Battles, William L. Adam, Isaac Porter, Charles Leo Preisker, Charles Bradley, Cary Calvin Oakley, Francis Marion Bryant, Martin Luther Tunnell and William D. Smith. They came for a chance to own land and to prosper greatly in the traditional American way. Many had tried mining for gold or silver or fur trapping or had established hotels, smithies, saloons or general merchandise stores in boom towns, but ultimately what they sought was the tried-and-true measure of a successful life, a place of their own to call home.

In the 19th century, the United States was a nation of mostly farmers. It was a time when agriculture and food availability predominated every aspect of life. In 1840, agriculture was nearly 70% of the labor force and had only declined to 58% in 1870 with the advent of labor saving inventions. Farms were an American way of life with land the prime ingredient. The search for open, available, arable land was the quest of most red-blooded males. It was a man's world, and women were still relegated to the kitchen and the bedroom. After the American Civil War, a few brave females were appearing in the workforce and escaping the family farm. Nursing and teaching were welcoming women into a new world, but it was on the homestead that women were still making the biggest impact, and it would be their children who will be the backbone of our great expanding nation.

Chapter Two: Santa Maria Pioneers

Elizabeth Conner Adam (1839-1898)

The year 1869 marked the arrival of one of Santa Maria's foremost pioneers, William Laird Adam. Previous to reaching the valley, in 1861 he met and married a Canadian girl, Elizabeth Conner in the Pajaro Valley, Santa Cruz County, California. Known as Bessie, she had arrived from Quebec by way of the Isthmus of Panama. The first five Adam children were born in either Santa Cruz County or Salinas, Monterey County.

Left to Right (back): Kenneth, James, Isabel, William C., Mary C., Charles (front): Anastasia, **Elizabeth Connor Adam**, Carlyle, Annie, Annie, William Laird Adam, Katherine, Thomas

Source: Memoirs of William Laird Adam

There were only about 100 people living in the valley when they arrived in the Santa Maria Valley. The Adam family settled on 160 acres near the river. Arriving with a herd of cattle, they started building a house immediately, completing it on Thanksgiving Day. Bessie's greatest desire, after a roof over her head, was for readily available water. Hauling water had plagued many valley families, but Bessie would not be so encumbered. The digging of a water well culminated on Christmas Day.

The Adam family was indeed industrious and prosperous. They seemed to be on a strict timeline: move the family, get settled, open a business. By the time the youngest child arrived in 1886, Bessie had birthed twelve children. The last of her children arrived when Santa Maria was still known as Central City. In 1888 Bessie and husband financed the planting of gum trees by James Goodwin in

Chapter Two: Santa Maria Pioneers

an effort to stop the untamed winds that raced across the valley. Adam would also support and advocate for the Agricola School, the East Main Street School and Santa Maria Union High School. He was director and president of the Santa Maria Valley Packing Company, president of the Bank of Santa Maria and president of the Santa Maria Water Company. He is also credited with chairing the committee that persuaded Union Sugar Company to locate in the valley.

The Adam family was heavily invested in real estate. They never sold a property once they purchased it. In consequence, they were the owners of at least ten large ranches as well as much valuable town property. Their plans for prosperity were coming to fruition.

Not much is known about Bessie other than that she would be grandmother to many future Santa Maria Valley families. Her son James married Mary Donovan, Charles married Jane Porter, Isabelle married Patrick Sheehy, Anastasia married Isaac Porter, Annie married Leo Preisker, Katherine married Joe Rembusch, Thomas married Grace Thornburgh and Carlyle married May Lafferty! All of these names are associated with the foundation of Santa Maria and many of her descendants are still present today. At a minimum the names of many of them adorn our streets. Bessie died at age 59; her legacy was a life well lived and well loved.

William Laird Adam (1836-1903)
m.(11/186) **Elizabeth Connor** (1838-1898)
    William Adam (1861-1944)
    Mary Adam (1863-1939)
    Isabell Adam (1864-1931)
    James Adam (1865-1910)
    Charles Adam (1867-1923)
    Thomas Adam (1870-1940)
    Anastasia Adam (1871-1954)
    m.(1899) Isaac Porter (1871-1937)
        Elizabeth Porter (1900-1991)
        m.(1936) Donald Prentice (1905-1998)
            Mary Prentice (-)
            John Prentice (-)
        Rose Porter (1901-1995)
        William (Bunny) Porter (1908-1993)
        m.(1937) Josephine Poncetta (1910-1983)
            Anastasia Porter (-)
            Isaac Porter (-)
            Rosemary Porter (-)
            Charles Porter (-)
    Margaret Adam (1873-1877)
    Kenneth Adam (c.1874-1899)
    Katherine Adam (1876-1928)
    Carlyle Adam (1881-1952)
    Anna Adam (1886-1959)

William Laid Adam family.

> The William Laird Adam family tree includes two of our ladies, **Elizabeth Connor Adam** and **Anastasia Adam Porter**.
> *Source: "California Central Coast Pioneer Families" by Barbara Cole. Used with permission of the Santa Maria Valley Genealogy Society.*

Elizabeth Booth Bradley (1840-1903)

Elizabeth Booth was born in South Wingfield, Derbyshire, England. She and Charles Bradley married in 1860 and immigrated via the steamer *"Colorado"* to San Francisco in November 1868. Elizabeth packed up her housewares and sailed with five children. They then traveled by boat from San Francisco to Monterey where Charles' Uncle Paul and Aunt Elizabeth welcomed the seven of them. Charles was answering a call from his uncle, Paul Bradley, to help with moving livestock to the Santa Maria Valley. After outfitting themselves with wagons, horses and other necessities, they set out south. It was quite the journey as the family walked the 160 miles with a herd of sheep; meanwhile, Elizabeth gave birth *en route* to a baby girl.

Elizabeth Booth Bradley
Source: Santa Maria Valley Historical Society collection.

The Bradley caravan must have framed quite the picture with children, sheep and covered wagon bouncing along. There was also a spring wagon loaded with household equipment and, behind it, a wheelbarrow loaded to capacity with an iron cook stove. Anyone who followed must have wonder what could have created that single wavering wheel track through the sandy wilds from Monterey to Central City (Santa Maria). The Bradley family carried on to a site that from that day to this, has been called Bradley Canyon.

The Bradley flocks and crops flourished, and they continued to purchase more land. In not too many years, the young English couple who came to America with five children and five dollars was destined to be one of the most prosperous land-owning pioneer blood lines in the valley. Their children would subsequently enjoy an additional perk on their 2,720 acres: oil, which would be discovered 23 years after Charles and Elizabeth Bradley's deaths.

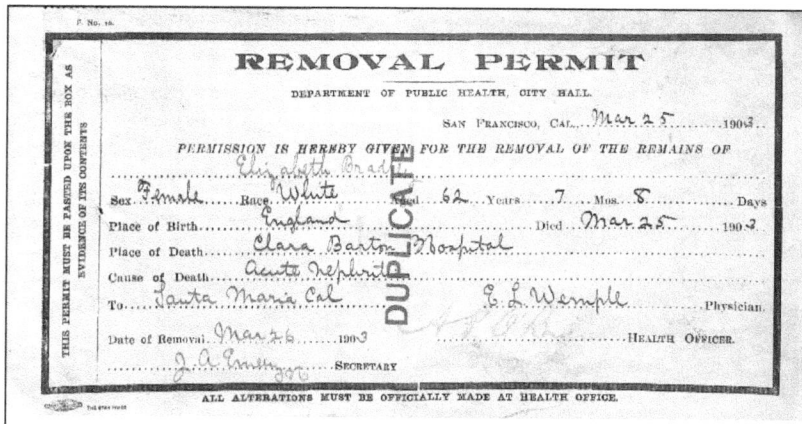

Elizabeth Booth Bradley died in San Francisco, and her body was transported to Santa Maria for burial.
Source: Dudley Mortuary artifacts donated to the Santa Maria Valley Historical Society.

Perhaps one of the most memorable investments the Bradleys' made was the purchase of the Hart House Hotel. Shortly after the change in ownership, it became known as The Bradley Hotel. It sported all the glitter and glam of the "Gay 90s."

In July 1939 the Bradley descendants held their first family reunion. There were 69 of the family present including seven of nine Bradley sisters. The Bradley girls married into other prominent pioneer families: Long, Miller, Tunnell, Goodchild, Calderon, Rubel and Bello. Descendants of Elizabeth are still in the Santa

Chapter Two: Santa Maria Pioneers

Maria Valley, and there is a major street bearing the Bradley name. Like many women of her day, Elizabeth reported on the last census taken before her death that her occupation was "housekeeping." If we pause to think of all of the things that would have been represented by the term "housekeeping," it is such an understatement as a summation of her life and who she was to generations to come. How many of twenty-first century women would whittle down her belongings, saving only a few pots and pans, and gather her five children to follow her husband, with nearly no cash, onto a boat that would have to navigate through the Straits of Magellan to reach its destination and then walk behind a wagon for 160 miles while pregnant? Elizabeth Bradley, more than "housekeeper" could ever describe, like many of her time, was a brave adventurer exploring a whole new world, making a life for her family and preparing a way and standard of living for generations.

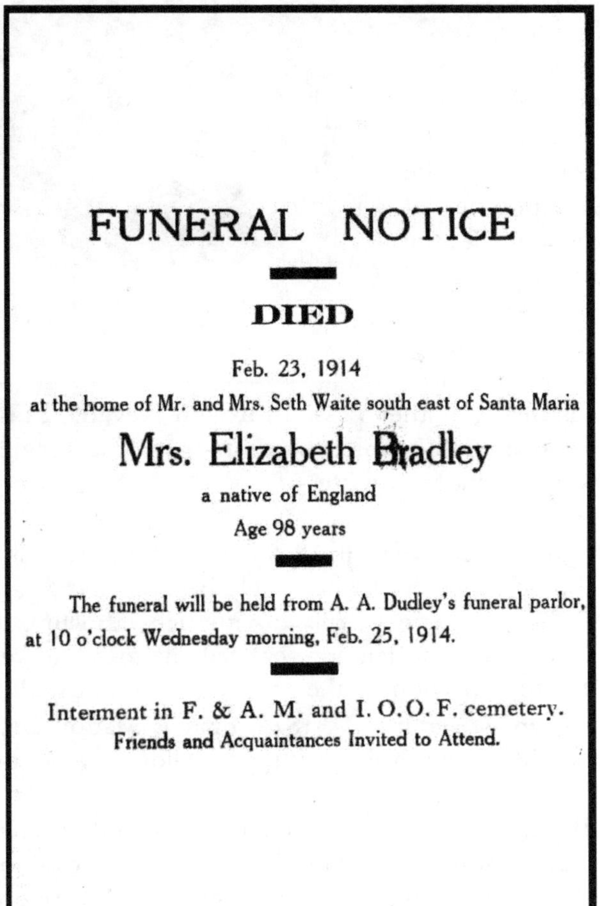

FUNERAL NOTICE

DIED

Feb. 23, 1914
at the home of Mr. and Mrs. Seth Waite south east of Santa Maria

Mrs. Elizabeth Bradley

a native of England
Age 98 years

The funeral will be held from A. A. Dudley's funeral parlor, at 10 o'clock Wednesday morning, Feb. 25, 1914.

Interment in F. & A. M. and I. O. O. F. cemetery.
Friends and Acquaintances Invited to Attend.

Elizabeth Bradley Funeral Notice
Source: Dudley Mortuary artifacts donated to the Santa Maria Valley Historical Society.

Elizabeth Spencer Bradley, the sister-in-law, of Elizabeth Booth Bradley, died on February 23rd. She was buried two days later, on February 25th. It was common for a person to be buried within a day or two of the day they died because there was no way to preserve the body beyond that. Newspapers, on the other hand, were typically weeklies. This meant that a person usually died and was buried before an announcement or obituary could be printed in the newspaper, so friends and relatives would not learn about the funeral until after it was past. The solution was to print handbills, as seen here. These were posted on poles and walls, or inside the post office and local businesses in order to facilitate getting the word out about the funeral.

Abigail Trott Bryant Wiley (1840-1924)

Abbey, as she was known to her family, was born in Bangor, Penobscot County, Maine, in 1840. At age 16 she married Francis Marion Bryant, also of Maine. She, her new husband and her family, the Trotts, headed for the Minnesota Territory and were part of the 1857 United States territorial census. Her youngest brother, George Joseph Trott, was born there in St. Anthony Falls, a big lumber and milling area that is today part of Minneapolis. Although Francis Bryant was a farmer, by 1860 he, like many before him, had decided to try his luck in the gold fields to the west. Traveling by covered wagon overland to Washoe, Nevada, for the next four years he tried unsuccessfully to "hit the jackpot." With little to show for their effort, Abbey and Francis returned with their children to Minnesota. It wasn't long before they began preparation to make a different kind of trek west. While the talk of gold and silver penetrated all parts of the continent, there was also talk of available land for those willing to homestead. Early wagon trails took a number of different routes. Some along northern paths and some, like the Bryants, were ferried across the Missouri River at Council Bluffs, Iowa. They had heard that the Oregon routes were often snowed in and the wagons abandoned. Having spent many winters in Minnesota, the southern route was probably

Abigail Trott Bryant Wiley
Source: Santa Maria Valley Historical Society collection.

the easiest choice among their preparations. Plans made, as they passed through Nevada, Frances Bryant still couldn't resist one more effort to strike it rich before succumbing to the inevitable conclusion that farming was the more likely pathway to a successful life.

Abigail Trott Bryant Wiley
Source: Santa Maria Valley Historical Society collection.

The Bryants settled on their farm in 1869 in a location that was one mile west and one-mile south of what would become known as the "four corners." Tales of a new village with rich farmland, ideal climate, and schools for the children enticed them to the valley. Today, in 2019, this location is the intersection of Stowell and Blosser Roads. On November 29, 1872, Francis Marion **Bryant** died at the age of 42, leaving Abbey with four children on her own.

Abigail Trott Bryant was a capable woman with boundless energy; she was kindly and devoted to her family and church. It was noted, but bore little-to-naught on her way of life, that she had been born with one leg shorter than the other, causing her to limp when she walked. She was so robust all of her days that no one took much notice of her condition, and it never created any kind of real impediment to her life.

In 1875, Abbey married Benjamin Wiley, the first settler in the Santa Maria Valley and twelve years her senior. He had been a widower most of his days in the valley. The energetic Abbey and her brood must have enchanted him for the long-widowed bachelor married her and moved them all to his farm near La Graciosa. Together, they had three sons, making seven children in the farmhouse. Her children would remember fondly that she always cooked family dinner on Sundays; that the kitchen, which was big, always smelled like a bakery, and there was always something wonderful cooking in the oven.

Abbey's son, Emmett Bryant, got his first real job in Central City in the general store owned by James F. Goodwin. Young Bryant had never wanted to be a farmer; it was his dream to work as a merchant. By 1880 a partnership was formed, and the store became Goodwin and Bryant Mercantile and Post Office. This was the beginning of the hardware business that, for the Bryant family, would last over 100 years. In 1890, Emmett Bryant and his uncle, George Trott, opened Bryant and Trott, which remained in business until July 1991.

Bryant and Trott Hardware, c. 1909.
Source: Santa Maria Valley Historical Society collection.

Abigail Trott Bryant Wiley was widowed again in 1902. She lived on until 1924, to the age of 84.

Mary Long Rice (1836-1936)

Mary Long was born in Ross County, Ohio, in 1863. A notorious tomboy, she shunned the feminine arts and preferred working with horses and laboring out of doors. She road sidesaddle most proficiently and enjoyed hunting and fishing. One of 12 children, at 17, she and her family joined with some other likeminded folks and caravanned their way to California in an ox-drawn prairie schooner. To ensure an adequate food supply, the travelers drove a herd of cattle along with them. Mary, being an expert horsewoman, was assigned responsibility of helping with the animals.

Mary Long Rice gravestone
Source: www.findagrave.com

Mary's riding and management of the cattle drew the attention of an Indian chief who offered six choice ponies for her. It created quite the anxious moment, but her father managed to politely turn down the "generous" offer. However, encounters with Indians didn't always turn out so well. Not long after turning the proposal aside, a young boy in the schooner train shot an elderly Indian woman who was fishing on the river bank near their encampment. What happened next haunted Mary's memories the remainder of her entire life. As the boy had killed the old Indian woman merely for sport, the Indians approached the travelers and demanded the 15-year-old be handed over to them for his callous, unthoughtful action. Fearing reprisals against the entire caravan, and having already refused to trade Mary, the decision was rendered to surrender the boy as commanded. He was taken across the river where the Indians all but immediately burned him alive. The caravan moved forward hoping that all debts were paid.

Mary Long Rice, seated, and Patty Boyd, next to her.
Source: Santa Maria Valley Historical Society collection.

Upon reaching Healdsburg, California, Mary met 17-year-old John Henry Rice. He had come to California by mule train to join the gold rush. Disappointed with his lack of good fortune, Rice was planning to farm. They married in 1854 and began farming in Sonoma County before moving to Salinas, California.

Chapter Two: Santa Maria Pioneers

In 1873, the Rices, now a family with four children, having heard rumors that there was plentiful land and resources, moved to the Santa Maria Valley where they again began farming. They built a home and dug a well before planting their crops. A roof over their head, plentiful water and supportive neighbors was the start of all good things for them. Originally settling on leased property west of Santa Maria, they later purchased a portion of the old Punta de la Laguna Rancho near Guadalupe. Although they had plenty, Mary's existence was a struggle. In addition to the regular chores of cooking at the fireplace, baking, washing and making clothes, she helped build fences and did other seemingly masculine chores. Her day began at 2 a.m. preparing breakfast for the men in the family who hauled grain from the valley to schooners at Point Sal. Being capable at the hearth and the fields had its drawbacks! Mary bore up well under her responsibilities.

Mary Long Rice
Source: Santa Maria Valley Historical Society collection.

When the Rice family had made enough money from crops to pay off the loan on the property, they sent their oldest son, William, to San Francisco with the gold from the sale of those crops. He took the stagecoach north; all the while the family anxiously awaited his return. Stagecoach robberies were common, and there was no insurance to protect passengers from losses. Fortunately, all went well for them, and the debt was paid. William returned safely.

Although her life was a rugged one, in her later years Mary would comment that "I have never faced anything which made me want to quit and die."

Mary Ann (Grandma) Rice.
Source: Santa Maria Valley Historical Society collection.

Mary Rice did more traveling than most pioneer women of her day. She traveled to Los Angeles twice, visited her husband's parents in Tennessee with him, and made trips to San Francisco on the narrow-beamed steamships that cruised along the coast calling at Port San Luis.

Mary was widowed in 1897 when she was 61 years old. Maintaining her independence, she remained in her own home at 715 S. Lincoln, watering her garden and trimming the flowers. She rose each morning at 6 a.m. and drank coffee three times a day. Mary's longevity earned this vibrant, energetic, athletic girl with the unconquerable spirit the moniker, Grandma Rice. Many articles were written about Grandma Rice in the 1930s as she reached her 9th decade. Those who knew her were only mildly surprised that this venerable grandmother had been a free-spirited wild plains girl in her youth, riding sidesaddle across the untamed, and then unnamed, states to find her way to California. She had witnessed the growth of the valley, the birth of a town and transformation of a state. In 1932 Marion B. Rice, her grandson became Mayor of the city of Santa Maria. Mary lived six days short of her 100th birthday.

Harriett Sharp Hart (1844-1896)

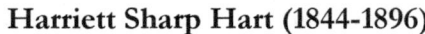

Harriet Sharp Hart
Source: Santa Maria Valley Historical Society collection.

Harriet was born in England in 1844, one of four children of Samuel and Hannah Sharp. At age 18, she made an unhappy and miserable marriage which she reportedly regretted every minute of every day. Harriet's marriage to Wilson Blood was a tumultuous one and would influence many of her life's decisions. England itself was in a time of turmoil and unrest. According to the Church of England, divorce was a sin. Harriet found herself married to a tyrannical, overbearing Englishman who was harsh and unjust in his treatment of her, yet she had no legal recourse. Harriet, already disenchanted with the rule of law in England, despised the social inequality between men and women. Only men could inherit and were virtual kings of the household; women were mere chattel. She had two daughters during this trying period, Laura Wilson Blood and Lucy Armitage Blood. Driven by intolerable conditions, Harriet with her parents, siblings and two daughters left England in the spring of 1868.

Harriet Sharp would never mention the name Wilson Blood again. Her horrific experience behind her physically, it would still persuade her life choices and political views in the United States. Once in America her family settled first in Delaware and then in Pennsylvania where Harriet was finally able to be divorced from Wilson Blood. Determined to put the entire imbroglio behind them, she and her daughters took her maiden name of Sharp.

Harriet wanted to be able to guide her own destiny. She had children to care for and her parents were aging. She was a single woman with responsibilities and few career paths to choose from. Harriet decided to go west where there were more opportunities for women.

While Harriet was gathering her strength and independence, her mother Hannah Armitage Sharp died. This opened the opportunity for Samuel Sharp to go to California with his daughter. Her girls remained with relatives in Pennsylvania while Harriet and her father assessed the possibilities out west.

Heading west in 1878 on the east-west railway system that had only been running for a few years, Harriet's move west was more comfortable and considerably safer than those who had gone shortly before her. It was certainly less challenging than those early years when California bound settlers walked behind covered wagons. Travel was still rugged and demanding, a woman seldom traveled alone. Perhaps this is why her somewhat frail father, Samuel Sharp, at age 61, ultimately decided to accompany his 34-year-old daughter.

Harriet began her California adventure in San Francisco. She established a sewing shop for a period of time then working for the White Sewing Machine Company as a travelling sales representative. In time, her business brought her to Central City, California, where she was charmed by the small but bustling little town. She decided to send for her daughters when she obtained a housekeeping position for one of its leading citizens, Reuben Hart, at his house on Bush and Broadway.

Harriet's girls were bundled up with a newlywed couple travelling on the Union Pacific Railroad. Laura turned 14 during the trek west; Lucy was 11 years-old. Arriving first in San Francisco, they eventually met their mother at Port Harford after a boat ride on the "Orizaba." Harriet drove out to her girls with a spring wagon, and they bounced their way along a rough road to a new life in Central City in late 1878. Both girls were soon registered to attend Pleasant Valley School.

As small towns are apt to do, there was talk about the handsome, industrious Reuben Hart and his housekeeper. On New Year's Eve 1878, Harriet married again. She and Reuben Hart held quite a big wedding ceremony and reception. It started raining and rained so hard that the wedding guests stayed and danced until dawn. The new family settled into the little house Harriet had been hired to keep, and, in October of 1881, Harriet Hannah (Hattie) Hart was born.

Harriet Sharp Hart
Source: Santa Maria Valley Historical Society collection.

In 1882 as Central City was transitioning to Santa Maria, her daughter Laura married Emmett Bryant, and in 1885 Lucy married William Haslam, III.

In 1888 the Harts opened the Hart House, an elegant hotel and showplace. Each suite of rooms had a fireplace and beautiful chandeliers. It was the jewel of Santa Maria. The Harts, with little Hattie, moved into the hotel for a time.

Harriet's life in America had given her a second chance at happiness; she was every bit the fervent suffragette with a quick wit and the mind to voice her opinions on women's economic and political rights. Harriet Hart became a charter member of the Ladies Literary Society, later named the Minerva Club. Harriet had often spoken out about how fortunate she was to have been able to have a second life; to bring her daughters to America and to find a husband who treated her as an equal. She was invited by the Society to give a speech to the group about women's issues. She began with a simple question to the ladies gathered, "Why is it men so fear the ballot of their wives and yet allow any disreputable man, be he drunkard, drug addict, or gambler, to vote and help make the laws that his wife and children must abide by, and yet in the city, this is the class of men who control the polls?" She spoke on exuberantly, releasing a lot of energy and frustration at what she deemed an unfair and illogical system.

The Hart home on Broadway and Church
Source: Santa Maria Valley Historical Society collection.

Chapter Two: Santa Maria Pioneers

The Harts lived in their elegant hotel for six years before moving to a little house on Broadway and Church. After moving to the home, Harriet at age 52 took ill with stomach cancer. She died on October 7, 1896. Her third daughter, Hattie, was only fifteen at her mother's passing but was left in the care of her loving father, Harriet's devoted husband.

Harriet Hart's life's legacy was as a major influencer to the valley women. In word and deed, she challenged them to take action in community issues they felt impacted the future of their families and their burgeoning town.

Hart Hotel (Hart House).
Source: Santa Maria Valley Historical Society collection.

Chapter Two: Santa Maria Pioneers

Source: Santa Maria Valley

Anna Van Valkenburg Blosser (1846-1926)

Anna Van Valkenburg Blosser
Source: Santa Maria Valley Historical Society collection.

Anna was born in Chatham, New York, in 1846 of Dutch descent. Garrett Van Valkenburg and Sarah Sedgwick Van Valkenburg emigrated to California in 1851 when Anna was five years old. They travelled by steamer down the east coast, crossed the Isthmus of Panama and came up to San Francisco. It was before the days of the railroad across the Isthmus. Adults crossed on mule back, while children were carried by natives. During Anna's crossing, some in their party got lost, and the reminder of the group had to wait all night in a native hut sleeping on skins on the floor.

Finally arriving in San Francisco, the Van Valkenburgs did not stay long but went directly to Stockton. Anna's father was a blacksmith and opened his own shop. When Anna was ten years old, her mother's hand was painfully afflicted, such that she could not use the hand for several months. Anna was taught to make bread, and she baked every bit that the family used. When the first California State Fair was held in Stockton the next year, Anna, at eleven entered a loaf of bread and won one of the women's department prizes for baking the best loaf of bread. It was a popular category, and a vast number of entries competed for the prize of $50 dollars. Anna was awarded this grand prize. Her parents took the $50 dollars and bought stock for her. A little disappointed, Anna had verbalized that her hope had been for a ribbon or medal that said BEST LOAF of BREAD. As she told her parents, "money is just money."

At age eighteen, Anna married Lorenzo W. Blosser in 1864. Her parents, father in particular, never liked California. Garrett Van Valkenburg longed for his old home back in New York. Her parents went back to a place near her childhood home, Chatham, New York, where they lived out their remaining years. They never returned to California, not even for a visit.

Anna's husband, like her father, was a blacksmith. Lorenzo and Anna decided on living in the Santa Maria Valley in 1869 and relocated to 160 acres of government land. A day or two after arriving, Anna and Lorenzo attended a party at the R.D. Cook residence. The festivity was to raise funds for the Pleasant Valley School. There were about 30 people attending. In their mid-twenties, the young couple could see a future need for a school and very much enjoyed the hospitality of their new home.

Pleasant Valley Schoolhouse
Source: Santa Maria Valley Historical Society collection.

When the Blossers arrived on their homestead, there was no house and no water. The lumber was on the ground waiting. Putting up the house was nothing compared to the hardship of hauling water. They began by lugging it from the Suey Ranch, where there was a well at the stage station. This was nearly six miles away. Two barrels were loaded in the back of the farm wagon to transport the water to the homestead. It took several months to dig the well, as it went down 65 feet. Pulling water up with a rope and bucket was an arduous task, but easier than transporting it from Suey Ranch Stage Station.

Anna shared some comments on her life as a pioneer's wife in her later years. She reported that there were drawbacks. "Frequently, my husband was compelled to leave me and the children alone on the ranch. It was a half-mile to the nearest neighbors. Those were lonesome times." She further went on to recall an incident when a swarthy man who had been drinking came to the ranch during one of her husband's absences. She was forced to bar the door and cautioned all her children to be quiet and hide. "We were trembling and scarcely dared to breathe while he tried to break in. Finally, he gave up and went away. I don't know what he wanted." Clearly life in the valley was not completely civilized. It was still the frontier. A woman had to be shrewd, careful and judicious.

Anna was very active in the work of her church. She helped to establish each of the three Methodist churches in Santa Maria. The latest Methodist church was erected in 1878 on Broadway, the lumber for it hauled here from the wreck of a ship that went down on the rocks at Point Sal. Preceding this church were two other Methodist churches on Church Street. Anna was a charter member of the Methodist Church Society, formed in 1873. At her eulogy, the Reverend George B. Cliff, pastor in charge, preached a most touching sermon declaring Anna had a long, Christian life of influence in her community.

The first Methodist Church, located on Church Street
Source: Santa Maria Valley Historical Society collection.

Margaret McHenry Tietzen (1859-1946)

Margaret, affectionately called Margie, was born to James Timothy McHenry and Sarah D. Pierce on 10 February 1859 in the city of Santa Rosa, California. Margie's mother died at age 35 when Margie was about 10 years old. Sarah gave birth to her fifth child, dying ten days after the birth of a son William, who survived until October of the same year, 1868.

Margie McHenry was well educated; she acquired her principal education in private schools and at the age of fourteen she began studying at Hesperian College in Woodland. A Disciples of Christ school, it was the first one to be organized in California. Current day Chapman University traces its lineage through Hesperian College. By age seventeen, Margie was teaching school in Yolo County. She was still living there at age 20 in 1880 with her father and his second wife and children.

As a young woman, Margaret became interested in temperance which meant to her and others in the movement; abstinence from alcoholic drink. She also was interested in other social changes or reform movements: education reform, prison reform, and women's rights.

The tendencies she had toward these reforms strongly marked her throughout her life. While still in her early teens, Margie, with several girlfriends, gave entertainments to fundraise on behalf of opening the Vallejo Orphan Asylum. The orphanage developed into a beautiful three-story building and stood for nearly 50 years. Located in once rural North Vallejo, it admitted more than 4,500 boys and girls until its closure in 1919.

In the fall of 1880, Margie came to San Luis Obispo where she taught school for several years. On November 14, 1883, Margie McHenry married Paul Otto Tietzen, a Prussian immigrant eight years her senior. Paul and Margie married in Guadalupe, California at the home of Dr. and Mrs. W. T. Lucas. There would be four children born to them. A son Paul Julius, named for his father and paternal grandfather, would not survive his first year. The other children: Ida, Hazel and Herbert, would reach adulthood.

Paul with Tietzen seated on the right with Margaret in the center. Daughter Ida is present behind Margaret husband and children.

Source: Santa Maria Valley Historical Society collection.

Margie was an ardent volunteer on behalf of the Christian Church. She devoted much of her time to the interests, missions and projects of her church, but was not confined to those sectarian paths alone. Being a woman of fine presence and character, a force in the community of Santa Maria, she worked tirelessly to bring before the ladies of the Santa Maria Valley information on the reform movements during her nineteen years as a resident of Santa Maria. As the wife of an extremely successful business man (P.O. Tietzen is credited with making the Bank of Santa Maria a success through some very chaotic financial time), she had a prominent position in Santa Maria and her perspectives, persuasions and words presented with a lot of prestige in the community. The population of Santa Maria in 1890 was 300.

Margie Tietzen was a strong advocate of temperance, a friend indeed to the poor and a pronounced suffragist. She was a very forceful speaker and lecturer on the platforms of suffrage and drink. It was also locally acknowledged that she was a writer of remarkable ability. Her stance on affairs of public interest was well known and her home on South Broadway, the scene of many gatherings.

Tietzen home on Claremont Boulevard
Source: Santa Maria Valley Historical Society collection.

During Margie's time in the valley she worked diligently, dedicating her time to push for the betterment of her community and the larger political conversations of her time. The greatest part of her life was dedicated to bringing forward her view of equality of opportunities. Margie Tietzen could be considered one of the first grand dames of Santa Maria. While the Tietzens enjoyed great success in Santa Maria, like others who had a big impact on the development of the valley, the Goodwins and the Blochmans, they moved on to bigger locales and continued to develop and experience great fortune. Paul built Margie and the family a mansion, which was under construction from 1910-1913 in Berkley at 2840 Claremont Boulevard. They also had a summer home in Pozo where they vacationed frequently with their great friends, the J.F. Goodwins. Margie would enjoy international travel and live long enough to witness prohibition, the Great Depression, World Wars I & II and perhaps most importantly, the right to vote.

Margaret McHenry Tietzen
Source: Santa Maria Valley Historical Society collection.

Margie passed at the age of 87 in her home in Berkeley and is buried in Oakland, California.

Anastasia Adam Porter (1871-1954)

Anastasia was known as Nessie. She was born in Central City, California, in 1871. The daughter of William Laird Adam and Elizabeth Conner, Nessie was one of 12 children. Nessie grew up in the brand new town of Santa Maria. Her family, arriving in 1869, was the 12th pioneering family to arrive. Her father William Laird Adam would become one of its foremost citizens.

Nessie received her schooling at the Agricola School and the Main Street School in Santa Maria before graduating from Immaculate Heart Convent in San Luis Obispo. Nessie married Isaac James Porter in 1899 at the Adam ranch house. They lived on the two-square-league (about 14,000 acres) ranch in Huasna Valley, part of the original land granted in 1843 by the Mexican government to Isaac's maternal grandfather Isaac James Sparks. Isaac's mother was Maria Rosa Sparks, one of three daughters who inherited the ranch. She married Arza Porter about 1869. Isaac James Porter was the oldest son.

Porter house at 519 S. Broadway as it is today.
Source: Santa Maria Valley Historical Society collection.

The Porter ranch home was more luxurious than many homes in town, but it was almost 20 miles from civilization. Nessie found the move from the modern improvements of city life to the wilds of ranch life to be a challenge. To reach the home from town, the trip was by horse-and-buggy or wagon. The road wound up the river; when there was water in the river, you couldn't reach the house from town or go into town if you were at the house. This situation would pose a continuous frustration. To breach the loneliness of ranch life, Isaac took his young wife to dances in the town of Huasna, roughly 40 miles along Suey Creek from Santa Maria. At the time, the town of Huasna was a thriving village, serving the countryside for miles around with a general store, post office, school and the Tail-Twist Saloon. Nessie once confided that she was shocked to find ranchers and vaqueros on the dance floor wearing guns and holsters, usually one on each hip!

Nessie had three children, two girls and a boy. She was a charter member of the Catholic Daughters of Santa Maria and of the Altar Society of St. Mary's. She was also a member of the Minerva Club.

The couple made their home on the ranch until 1908 when son William Arza Porter was born, then the family established a home in Santa Maria on South Broadway. Isaac continued to run cattle but maintained a town address, first at 403 S. Broadway, which is at the corner of Broadway and Cook Streets. The family move into their 519 S. Broadway home by 1920 thus forever ending their issue with the filling river bed. When it rained, they stayed in town! Living in town also made it easier for the children to attend high school.

Isaac died in 1937. Nessie lived into her 80s, and it has been reported that she haunts the 519 address where, in 2019, a chiropractic office is housed. Employees report seeing her in various rooms and the hallway of what has become commonly known in Santa Maria as the Porter House.

Ghost stories aside, Nessie Adam Porter was a bright, colorful character, leaving behind many proud descendants. Her son, William Arza "Bunny" Porter, married and raised a family on Rancho Huasna where family still resides.

Chapter Three: The Four Ladies of the Four Corners

Post-civil war America was fraught with both challenges and opportunities. All Americans found Reconstruction a time of social, economic, and political turmoil. Many people were relocating and, in so doing, escaped the uncertainty and bad memories of the evolving landscape that was the reunited states of America. Searching for new horizons unblemished by war, distrust and hatred, many made their way west. The Homestead Acts provided a chance for a whole new life. These "acts" were several laws by which an applicant could acquire ownership of land, a "homestead." The Homestead Acts opened up millions of acres. They gave new hope to many, both near and far, as folks already in the war-scarred states moved west and others across the pond found passage to our shores.

There were few requirements to satisfy to gain land ownership. Any adult who had never taken up arms against the U.S. government (no Confederates!) could apply if they met the following requirements: head of household or at least 21 years old, willing and able to live on the designated land, build a home, make improvements, and farm it for a minimum of five years (https://en.wikipedia.org/wiki/Homestead_Acts - cite_note-19). The filing fee was 18 dollars (a value equivalent to $270 in 2019). The Homestead Acts, and the excitement they inspired in many for a new beginning in a new place, helped to settle the West. It wasn't perfect as the acts were sometimes abused, but many prospered with the opportunity.

Early homesteaders in Suey Canyon, George Washington Battles and wife Rachel, 1868
Courtesy of Glenn Battles.

The early days of the Santa Maria Valley were founded by folks who were intent on finding open land to homestead. Filing for unclaimed land between granted ranchos in arable terrain was integral to starting a new life for many, and the Santa Maria Valley was a not-so-hidden treasure. Word was quickly spreading that there was a valley with room and prosperity awaiting. On arrival these adventurers also found that there were grasshoppers and gophers, dust and wind, but the opportunity was there if one could conquer the elements.

By general definition and like the land grants that preceded them, homesteading was an isolating and lonely existence. City girls were often lonesome for family and the bustle of more urban life. In the valley there were no trees in sight, and the morning fog was dense. Water had to be hauled over a distance, and there were few homes within a day's walk, so visiting a neighbor was not a regular occurrence. Isolation, loneliness and toil were words written into the journals of many. Yet, they found strength in a life devoted to family, faith, and town building.

The first settlement was by Benjamin Wiley in 1867. He employed a Mr. Norway, the county surveyor, to examine the location respective to the Spanish land grants. After a careful examination of the locality and search of deeds recorded in the county, the Santa Maria area was deemed safe to settle. It was a strip of government land 6 miles wide and 15 miles long.

Chapter Three: The Four Ladies of the Four Corners

Over the next few years, families began to arrive and thrive. There were more than a few difficult years with drought, red spiders, and fire, which were then compounded with unfortunate accidents and illness. Eventually, good fortune descended on the valley, and the town grew up

Man in wagon drawn with white mule in front
of early downtown business.
*Source: Santa Maria Valley
Historical Society collection.*

Chapter Three: The Four Ladies of the Four Corners

Minerva Marshall Maulsby Thornburgh (1820-1898)

The Religious Society of Friends began as a movement in England in the mid-17th century. Members became informally known as Quakers, as it was said they "tremble in the way of the Lord." The Quakers, though few in numbers, have been influential in the history of reform. Minerva Marshall was born into a prestigious and noted Quaker family. Her father was Miles Marshall. He was the head of one of six Quaker families who moved to Wayne County, Indiana, to avoid persecution by Puritans and to make a favorable life. The Quaker families of Wayne County were by arrival: the William family in 1814, Swain family in 1815, Marshall family in 1816, Maulsby family in 1817, Willis family 1817 and Thornburgh family in 1819. Minerva would eventually be connected to three of the six families.

Minerva Marshall Maulsby Thornburgh
Source: Santa Maria Valley Historical Society collection.

Minerva, or Nerva, as she was often called, was born in 1820 in Economy, Indiana. Farms were small: 100 acres, 80, even 40 sometimes. Women did their full share of work: spun raw cotton weaving it into clothing and raised flax, a food and fiber crop that they could turn into linen and make bedsheets and fine clothing. Younger girls did the cooking. Nerva Marshall was also a teacher for a short period.

Nerva Marshall married Dr. Ira C. Maulsby on March 31, 1839. Minerva was 19 years old, and Ira was 20. They lived on one of those small farms in Wayne County, Indiana. Ira had studied medicine and was a local physician as well as a farmer. Minerva would have been especially busy with a farm to care for and a husband who worked away. The additional responsibilities probably developed Minerva into a more independent woman. This became apparent when Nerva was disowned by her Quaker Meeting House for becoming a separatist in 1845. Younger Quakers were becoming a significant part of the movements for the abolition of slavery, for equal rights for women, and for peace. Minerva was part of this timeline when young Quakers had taken a stand, and she let her voice be heard.

A year later, in 1846, she and Ira had a son, Luna Marshall Maulsby. Unfortunately, their happiness was short lived. Four years later, in 1850, Ira contracted typhoid from a patient and left Nerva a widow at the age of 30. Now all the responsibility for the farm and her young son rested firmly on Nerva's shoulders.

Marriages of convenience were often contrived by couples for practical, financial, or political reasons. Sometimes the arrangement was made by families to provide very practical support for one or both parties. Whether Nerva's next marriage was a love match or arranged, it would endure.

John Thornburgh and Nerva Maulsby married February 23, 1859. She had been a widow for nine years. John had ten children, his first wife dying at age 32 in 1850. He was 50 years old to her 39 and suffered severely from asthma.

In 1862 they joined other Indiana Quaker families who were moving to Redfield, Iowa. Located on the edge of the frontier, the trip was 400 miles by horse and wagon. The American Civil War had

Chapter Three: The Four Ladies of the Four Corners

begun in April of 1861, and Indiana was a strong supporter of the Union. Indiana contributed approximately 210,000 Union soldiers, sailors, and marines. Iowa's contribution by contrast during the war was in providing food and supplies for the Union army as its contributions in manpower were overshadowed by larger and more populated eastern states.

Minerva Marshall Maulsby Thornburgh
Source: Santa Maria Valley Historical Society collection.

Despite their efforts to stand away from the war, Nerva and John found their sons fighting for the north, reflecting all the separatist beliefs except that last, peace.

A new marriage had given Nerva new purpose and a new and very large family, but her worries and losses were not over. The American Civil War would claim her only natural son with Ira Maulsby, Luna. He was destined to suffer and die in Andersonville prison camp at age 18 in July 1864. Her step-son, Henry Thornburgh, would also be sacrificed. He would die while serving with the 8th Regiment, Indiana Cavalry.

Nerva's husband, John continued to suffer severely from asthma. Stories had been drifting back to Iowa about the wonderful climate in California. Nerva, stricken with the pain and losses suffered from the war and not wishing to become a widow again, she and John made a plan to help John find a more comfortable climate to soothe his condition. With Nerva's encouragement, John forged ahead to California and in 1869 took up a claim in Ventura County on the ocean side of Rincon Hill, high on the mesa; in 1870 Nerva joined him. She traveled in considerable comfort aboard the new Central Pacific Railroad to San Francisco. The transcontinental line had just been opened. John was doing better, but not great. After only a year, once again they decided to change their location and started for Santa Cruz. It was there that they met R.D. Cook, who persuaded them to locate on government land in what would be known as the Santa Maria Valley. In 1871, John, at age 62, instructed Nerva to pack up their goods and prepare for yet another move. Once again the Thornburgh family joined with other pioneers, this time trying their luck post-Civil War in the treeless, dry, wind-blown and dusty valley that neither the Spanish and Mexican governments couldn't even give away. It was federal land and open for homesteading, and the climate was promising to a suffering John Thornburgh.

By the time John and Nerva had arrived in the valley, John didn't expect to live very long. His asthma was depriving him of strength and surrounded by his loving family, John just wanted to settle down for what he considered his last days. Much to their surprise, good fortune finally smiled down on John and Nerva Thornburgh. The central coast climate was very soothing and healing to his chronic condition. He improved daily and so remarkably that he would live another 21 years.

Cook had encouraged the Thornburgh family to move to the Valley, and it would be his brother Larkin Cook's land that John would purchase. Larkin had purchased it from Wat Rodenburg, a man who accidently shot himself to death while hunting. Larkin fell to ill health and subsequently died. This land was made available again, by tragedy. John paid $500 for 160 acres which included part of

Chapter Three: The Four Ladies of the Four Corners

what is now the southwest corner of Main and Broadway. The land proved good for the Thornburghs.

The last corner was now in place for the little town that would become Santa Maria. First, it would go through many changes. It is a square mile in the flattest, dustiest part of the Valley plain and owned by four farmers, each with 160 acres. In 1874, there are 12 families living in the immediate area. This influx, created the opportunity for these four families to come together and lay out a town site. John and Nerva Thornburgh contributed 40 acres into the project that would be Santa Maria. The other three families participating were the Millers, Cooks and Feslers.

A town was born, and John and Nerva settled down to farming and running the Grange store. Nerva, no longer the young separatist of Indiana, was a woman who was older than most of the new wives arriving and who was considered the motherly type. She was well liked and generous, donating the land on which to build the first Methodist church on the northeast corner of Church and Lincoln. In 1872 the first cemetery had been established by the Thornburghs at the corner of Broadway and Boone, mostly out of necessity as both Wat Rodenburg and Larkin Cook had been buried there on the property they had once owned.

> One unintended contribution that is ironically attributed to John and Nerva Thornburgh, who were ardent teetotalers, is Whiskey Row. Siding with the "drys," they did not allow any alcohol in their quarter-section. This decision created the environment for all the drinking establishments to line up on "the other corner" where Isaac Miller had no issue with drink.

John and Nerva were a friendly and social pair. They took in roomers and boarders mostly for the excitement that visitors brought. In their parlor in the evening, they entertained by having different people read aloud to anyone who wished to join them. The town proper was approximately 200 people in 1880.

Minerva in front of the Thornburg house in Santa Maria
Source: Santa Maria Valley Historical Society collection.

Nerva was always well loved and esteemed. She was energetic and intelligent all of her years, bearing up under her losses. She personally welcomed all the new ladies who came to town, inviting them to her home. Slowly a group began to meet regularly in her parlor.

John died in December of 1892, more than 20 years beyond the first dire prognosis he received, his respiratory system finally tuckered out according to Doc Lucas who diagnosed pneumonia as his cause of death. John died quietly in his favorite armchair at the age of 83. Nerva died six years later in 1898 afflicted with catarrh of the stomach, a very painful and difficult condition. She was 78 years old. Shortly after her death, the Ladies Literary Society would be renamed the Minerva Library Club. This club is still active today in 2019.

Mary Nancy Barnes Fesler (1822-1895)

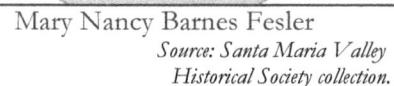

Mary Nancy Barnes Fesler
Source: Santa Maria Valley Historical Society collection.

Nancy Barnes was born in Tennessee, February 12, 1822. Her parents were James and Mary Polly Watkins Barnes. James Barnes was born in North Carolina in 1801. Like many early Americans, the Barnes' moved around looking for something better for their family. They were the eighth family to arrive in Derry Township near El Dara, Pike County, Illinois, in the early 1830s. Nancy met the Kentucky born Isaac Fesler in Derry Township, Illinois. They were married in October 1841 in Griggsville, Illinois, a town some 15 miles distant from El Dara. The first four Fesler children were born in Illinois around Pleasant Vale Township before the family moved to Linneus, Missouri, in the spring of 1855, where they would remain to farm for the next ten years. In that time three more children were born.

Like many before him, Isaac Fesler decided to take his family west. Their trip to California in 1865 was a long and arduous one. Traveling by wagon train, with the older children walking most of the way, the Feslers first settled in Sonoma, then for several years in the Sacramento Valley, where the last child was born in 1869.

> Places like El Dara, Griggsville and Linneus were virtually frontier towns. Consisting of the bare amenities, these towns were mostly farming communities with very little infrastructure. There was land to toil over but not much else. Many Midwest families were moving further and further west. The tales of the west coast were exciting and inviting. Rich, fertile land was available, not to mention gold and other valuable minerals! Farmers were desperately needed to feed the miners and business people in the new state of California.

Hearing about the opportunity for a homestead with good farmland to the south, in the autumn of 1869, Isaac and Nancy again gathered their family and made a trek, this time to what would eventually become the Santa Maria Valley. Nancy was forty-seven years old.

Perhaps a lot had been learned as the Feslers trekked from small farming community to small farming community. On arriving in the Valley, they purchased the northwest section of what was to become Central City in just a few years. Isaac would eventually come to an agreement with three other homesteaders (Cook, Thornburgh, and Miller) to make available 40 acres to become one quarter of a new town. He would also contribute property on which the Security First National Bank would be built and property for the Pacific Coast Railroad right-of-way.

This time the Feslers were part of a burgeoning enterprise; the town took new life and grew and families moved closer together. The townspeople started having picnics, band concerts and other social events. Nancy had lost her first three children in 1869, 1871, and 1872, but with those losses behind her, her remaining children flourished and began to marry. Their descendants remain in the valley today.

Chapter Three: The Four Ladies of the Four Corners

Isaac died in 1891 at age 72, spending twenty-two years in the Santa Maria Valley. Nancy died at 73, in 1895, at the home of her oldest surviving son, Stephen A. Fesler. Her obituary read, "Mrs. Fesler was highly esteemed by all who knew her…she was devoted to her children and grandchildren."

Soure: http://hddfhm.com/clip-art/free-pioneer-clipart.html

Not much is known about Nancy Fesler other than that she was here. As today, in those days' obituaries were written about the old by the young. Their memories of the deceased were characterized mostly by their last days. The writer had no memory of the loved one as a young person. Still with some small amount of thought, what we know of Nancy Fesler is that she was like many of the frontier women of her time who traveled with their husbands, mostly on foot, thousands of miles across a vast, unsettled, sparsely populated terrain. She had made the brave decision to raise a family, participate in a community, and live life to its fullest, despite despair, in order to settle a country, build a state, and establish a town.

Chapter Three: The Four Ladies of the Four Corners

Anna Robrecht Miller (1838-1917)

Anna Robrecht was born in Prussia. An historically prominent German state, Prussia was located on the southeast coast of the Baltic Sea, more than 6,000 miles from California. Anna arrived on the east coast of the United States unable to speak any English. She also still had another 2,000 miles to travel before she would reach Isaac Miller. She and Isaac would marry in Winnemucca, Humboldt County, Nevada, May 29, 1864. It seems unlikely these two met by accident leaving one to speculate that this was an arranged marriage, but by whom, a newspaper or relatives? Like the Foxens, the Millers began their marriage without the benefit of understanding each other's languages. Eduarda Foxen had once told a friend, "there is a language of the eyes." Perhaps Isaac and Anna spoke that same language of love.

Affectionately called Annie, her journey to America was a no-frills adventure. She made the voyage on the steamboat *Teutonia* departing from Hamburg, Germany. Records show that she travelled as a 24-year-old unmarried woman with someone named August Robrecht, perhaps a brother or cousin who accompanied her to her destination. Her residence was listed as Herstelle, Prussia, with a departure date of 8 August 1863. She traveled in steerage, which was enormously profitable for steamship companies.

Anna Robrecht Miller
Source: Santa Maria Valley Historical Society collection.

> Even though the average cost of a ticket was only $30 (almost $1,000 by today's standards), larger ships could hold from 1,500 to 2,000 immigrants, netting a profit of $45,000 to $60,000 for a single, one-way voyage. The cost to feed a single immigrant was only about 60 cents a day! Passengers in steerage survived on tepid soups, black bread, boiled potatoes, herring and portions of stringy beef.
>
> Immigrants who arrived at the Port of New York from 1820 to 1892 landed at Castle Garden. The Emigrant Landing Depot at Castle Garden was established in 1855. From August 3, 1855, to April 18, 1890, Castle Garden was America's first official immigration center, a pioneering collaboration of New York State and New York City. In 1890, the federal government became determined to control all ports of entry and take responsibility for receiving and processing all immigrants to the U.S. The Castle was closed, and the reception center was moved to the U.S. Barge Office which was located on the eastern edge of The Battery waterfront. It operated until the U.S. Office of Immigration opened Ellis Island in 1892.

How Annie got from the east coast to Nevada is unclear. A clerk's note on her passage entry wrote, "Aug. Bolten Wm. Miller's Nachfolger." What this means is anybody's guess, but Star City, Nevada, is a long way from New York. However, it does suggest Annie traveled with a chaperone or at the behest of a Miller. She arrived at Castle Garden on August 27, 1863, and was married to Isaac within 9 months.

Isaac had "struck it rich" with silver in Nevada after years of small successes and failures. The strike was so big that a whole town was created, Star City, Nevada. It became a boom town filled with costly hotels, saloons, stores and quartz mills. The population was several thousand in 1863. The Star Mining District, including the Sheba Mine, produced $5 million in silver ore by 1868. Miller's personal value was such that, in 1863, he built a large hotel at a cost of over $25,000. The 1870 Census lists Isaac as a quartz miner and Annie as "housekeeping" with one child. Then, with the same fervor with which it exploded, the town disappeared.

Chapter Three: The Four Ladies of the Four Corners

Only 78 people were in residence a year later in 1871. In droves, wagons were loaded with all manner of housewares and goods and hit the trail. Eventually Star City was entirely abandoned and became a ghost town.

The Millers had family in the Santa Maria Valley, and, in 1873 they too abandoned Nevada and trekked the relatively short distance and settled down to farm in the Valley. Joel Miller, Isaac's brother, was teaching at Pleasant Valley School. His sister was Mrs. James Handy Harris; whose husband was one of the four original homesteaders in the valley. A brother, Dr. J.S. Miller, was a local physician. With the exception of one sister, who stayed in Santa Rosa, Annie and Isaac Miller's appearance in the Valley completed the reassembly of the extended Miller family's migration from Virginia.

Annie delivered a daughter, Minna, shortly after their arrival. Isaac went into partnership with William Lovett, opening a small store, which they operated for a short time before Isaac went on to plant fruit trees. The Millers planted 40 acres in apricots and were probably the first to plant fruit trees in the valley. They also had prunes and peaches. For many years, in the summer time, their farm was a great gathering place of old and young working alongside each other in the orchard picking and drying fruits. A draught year ended most of the fruit in the valley.

Six children were born to Annie and Isaac; one daughter and four sons survived to adulthood. Annie died in 1917 age 79, preceding Isaac in death although she was nearly eleven years younger. Isaac was 90 years, 7 months and 14 days at his death on January 8, 1919. The Great War must have been very emotional for Annie to hear about, and her death preceded the end of the war and the Treaty of Versailles, which would inevitable change her homeland forever.

The Miller Division of downtown became home to Whiskey Row, a notorious stretch avoided by proper ladies! Miller's stance on alcohol was that he had no objection to drink, as opposed to his partner, Quaker John Thornburgh. Miller's willingness to rent to certain businesses in his quadrant made his section along Main Street a magnet to pool halls, saloons, bars and rather shady hotels.

Ironically the street named for Miller bordering the town was predominately family homes and is now one of the main thoroughfares through the city of Santa Maria.

Whiskey Row, 100 block of East Main St., Santa Maria, CA
Source: Santa Maria Valley Historical Society collection.

Janetti Lillian Nelson Cook (1838-1896)

Janetti Lillian Nelson Cook
Source: Santa Maria Valley Historical Society collection.

Marriage was the foundation of a women's life in the 19th century. A lady of the Valley was recognized mainly by her married name. Women referred to each other as Mrs. Smith and Mrs. Jones. A husband gave enormous status. This leaves the historian to speculate along such lines as: "what influence did women have over their husbands?" and "Did women shape their husband's views on politics or religion?" The boisterous girls married by the hardworking men of the Valley didn't cease to be boisterous with marriage, but how they expressed themselves changed, at least in the beginning, until it seemed the men quit listening. A woman's first name did have a place, on legal documents mostly.

Netti Nelson, was born in Oakridge, Guilford County, North Carolina, on May 25, 1838. Her father's family, the Nelsons, had been in Virginia as early as 1749, and her great-grandfather, Alexander Nelson, was a patriot soldier in the American Revolutionary War. The family migrated to North Carolina, then Netti's father, John, headed west with his family to Richmond, Ray County, Missouri. When he died, in 1843, Netti was only five years old, and her mother remarried.

R.D. Cook, born in Ohio in 1832, was one of a family of fourteen. His father a carpenter and farmer, through total necessity sent his son off to be self-supporting at an early age. Young Cook headed out to Illinois at 19 intent on making his way to California. On April 1, 1850, he started across the continent with a large wagon train of sixty-four ox-drawn prairie schooners. There were 135 men, women, and children in the party. After four hard months, the wagon train arrived in the gold fields near Hangtown (today, Placerville). Cook moved on to Sonoma, arriving with only 75 cents in his pocket but tons of enthusiasm. He had a trade, carpentry. His goal was to find his own land, but the flood of men looking for the same thing pressured him into working his trade. He hadn't reached his 21st year and would need ready cash for a homestead anyway, so he worked his trade starting out at $5 a day, a week later, he was making $60 per week as a builder. Good fortune and hard work were preparing young Cook to achieve his goal.

> In Netti's case, her first name has been spelled at least five different ways. Netti being a nickname, it isn't even included in the count! Her headstone in the Santa Maria Cemetery has it chiseled in granite as Janetti. Her marriage certificate from Sonoma spelled it Jennetta, the land documents on record in Santa Barbara County spell it Jinetta at the top and Jinnetta at the bottom on the signature line. As you can imagine it appears in other places with either an a, an i, or an e in the front, and then we have the fun of deciding on one "n" or two and move from there to deciding on one "t" or two. You can also choose the last vowel as either an "i" or an "a." And you have all the variations that go with each vowel change and the single or double consonant. In *This is Our Valley*, her name was spelled Jinnetta. It is impossible to know what was her preference or deemed correct.

While Netti's future husband was working on his dream, her mother had married Joshua Lamb, and by 1850 all were living in Cashe Creek, Yolo County, California. There is no documented record of

Chapter Three: The Four Ladies of the Four Corners

how they made their way to California, but most likely it was by wagon train. Her step-father must have had an interest in gold but like many a man before him, he soon returned to farming and caravanned his family into Santa Rosa, California.

> In 1860 Santa Maria Valley was an unsettled plain inhabited by a very few. There were no roads to mark the path that travelers should take to reach a given location save a few trails worn in by the local indigenous natives who lived in the hills above Sisquoc. Untamed horses and wild hogs mingled with cattle and other animals that abounded in the Valley. The only means of communication was via the stage. Yet, there was available land, and that was worth everything.

In October 1854, Cook met and married Netti in Santa Rosa. He took up a claim but only briefly. Their first child was born and lived only a few months, a little boy, Eberly. Soon afterwards, in 1856, he sold out his claim and went to Missouri via the Isthmus of Panama. In Saint Charles County, Missouri, Cook organized a company of nine men (including three of his brothers: Larkin, Layfayette, and Othup) and taking 353 head of cattle and 20 horses, he headed back to California. He made the journey in 3 months and 15 days. He traded his stock for land and sheep, and the Cooks prospered until the dry year of 1864 when he lost in excess of $25,000, which was everything that they had. Netti and R.D. needed a new start. They were raising four little girls. So in 1869, the Cooks joined a wagon train *en route* to Los Angeles. They stopped in the Valley where a tract of government land was just opened for settlement. There were no houses available for the family in the area of the new homestead, but temporary shelter was made in the Old Adobe at Guadalupe with the Hunt family.

Having safely arrived but with no home, plans were made to put the Cook carpentry skills to good purpose. R.D. and his brother Larkin drove an eight-horse team using a jerk line, the men walking the whole way to haul lumber from Port Harford nearly 30 miles away. They built a two-story frame house, twenty-four feet long by sixteen feet wide with two rooms, one upstairs and one down stairs. Both brothers being very fond of society, they immediately opened their new house, located at what becomes Main and McClelland Streets, with a party and dance before moving in. With Joel Miller as Master of Ceremony, the Cooks hosted the first fundraiser for Pleasant Valley Schoolhouse. The school was built for $510 and mostly by Cook! The four Cook daughters were among the first 15 pupils to gather for instruction when school began with Uncle Joel teaching in February, 1870.

The Cook family, c. 1902 (left-to-right): Ella, Fred, Viola, John Tunnell, Rudolph, Mary; (front) Laro Jones, Therand Tunnell
Source: Santa Maria Valley Historical Society collection.

Chapter Three: The Four Ladies of the Four Corners

Janetti Lillian Nelson Cook
Source: www.findagrave.com

The Cook home was noted for its hospitality. Clearing the land, plowing and planting was the beginning. Constant dust storms and wind followed by plagues of gophers and grasshoppers challenged Valley farmers; still the Cooks kept out the welcome mat for visitors. Picnics, horseback riding and traveling by wagon after long work weeks kept the moods light and grateful. The Cook girls began to marry men in the valley: Mary Samantha married Milton Miller, Lillian Viola married Samuel Jefferson Jones, Martha Ellen married John Tunnell, and Emma Jinnetta married Barney DeVine. Probably the biggest surprise for the Cooks arrived in August of 1876 with the birth of a boy, Frederick Lee Cook, to Nettie and R.D. just as all of the girls were leaving the nest.

The Cook land was destined to be one of four corners of present-day Santa Maria. The family would participate in community life and work to build a thriving city. In 1874, Cook had the town laid out and started a blacksmith shop. Ruben Hart purchased propitiously located property for his Hart House Hotel moving the blacksmith shop to the back of the property. Cook then opened the Pioneer Stable.

The Cooks took part in many public enterprises that went for the betterment and development of the Valley. They enjoyed great success and prosperity until in 1896 when Nettie became ill. Dr. Paulding treated her for "ulcers of the stomach." Unfortunately, at age 58, in June of that year, Nettie passed away. R.D. would survive Nettie into the next century, passing in 1904, a year before Santa Maria would finally be incorporated.

Chapter Four: Town Builders

Imagine walking a thousand miles or more into an empty space with a group and making the decision to "settle." Arriving at a location that has been determined as your destination, one looks about, and the real estate is everything you want, but there is nothing for many miles around. Towns began with a handful of people taking up land in an area and then created a central location to establish commerce, build schools, schedule mail delivery, and erect churches. When we think of a colony on the moon or even Mars, the experience isn't that different from what our ancestors faced in settling the West or going back 400 years, to arriving in Jamestown, Virginia Colony.

Source: Santa Maria Valley Historical Society collection.

To survive, you must be able to provide yourself with food and shelter in a relatively unknown environment. Food must be cultivated with enough carried with you to cover a growing season; shelter must be built that can endure the rigors of any extreme conditions that might present. To build a town, one doesn't start with extras, like entertainment; however, a saloon was often the first edifice put up! Starvation or death from exposure sometimes took 90% or more of a population. That number was often compounded by communicable disease. As one historian pointed out however, it isn't so surprising that so many died as it is that so many lived! Under the worst conditions and deprivations of comfort, people prevailed in new, unchartered, undeveloped land.

A town was so much more than what we recognize it as today. A town was an extended family. The relationships were lifelong, even if life itself was short many times. To build a town, the members had to be all in; there was no halfway. The level of cooperation needed to successfully form a town was monumental and often times the people vastly different in many aspects, except for in the most important perspectives, which was to create safe, productive, and improved lifestyles for themselves and future generations. The goal of every town builder was a better life.

Mary Olive Earl Winters (1861-1946)

Mary was born in Ashton, Lee County, Illinois, to Duncan and Esther Earl on November 7, 1861. Her father had immigrated in the 1840s to Illinois from Canada. In 1857, he met and married her mother who was also originally from Canada. Duncan Earl registered for the draft during the American Civil War; however, he was 40 years old at the time and was not called up. In 1870, he lists himself in the census at Lee County, Illinois, as a laborer with three children: Robert, Mary and Elizabeth. In 1872, the Earl family is residing in Central City, California, after having first settled in Gilroy.

Mary Olive Earl Winters
Source: Santa Maria Valley Historical Society collection.

The Earls homestead was north of what is today Waller Park. At an early age, Mary, who was never idle a day in her life, became a teacher. She began her time as a teacher providing private lessons to the children of Eliza and Charles Clark in their home at Point Sal.

When she was nearly 17, she married John H. Winters on September 18, 1878. They owned a ranch east of Waller Grove near her parents. She had two children while living there. One evening while John was working away from the ranch, an armed bandit approached the house. Her younger brother was with her and the children when they were awakened by the intruder's exuberant, perhaps drunken, ebullience. They quickly made for the back door avoiding a confrontation with the man who would enter the house and eat heartily before leaving. Spending the remainder of the night at a neighbor's home, Mary soon insisted on some changes.

The Winters would move to Point Sal. During this time, three children would be born. Eventually, she would have seven children, with two dying as infants. The Winters moved once more, this time to "Section 8," Bradley Canyon. Luck was not on their side, and their ranch house caught fire leaving Mary severely burned. Not to be defeated, they rebuilt and began again.

John died in 1908, and Mary ran the 620-acre farm on her own. She rose early in the mornings, had her horse saddled and rode across the place overseeing all of the work. Finally, in 1910, she sold out and moved into Santa Maria. She bought the J.K. Triplett place, which was two acres at 801 S. Lincoln Street.

Living in town gave Mary the chance to become active in the Methodist Church that she cherished all of her life. She was a member of the Eastern Star and became a Matron of the organization. As soon as the Minerva Club formed, she became a member, later a president. She was also a member of the Santa Maria Valley Pioneer Association.

As the years passed, Mary stayed involved in her community. She was a member of the high school board of trustees for 25 years. It was her work with the school that gave her the greatest joy. Teachers and students alike sought her council, and she strove to support and inspire them.

During the Great War, her heart swelled with compassion for the combatants in the terrible conflict. She joined the American Red Cross and worked tirelessly for all activities in Santa Maria during the war. She helped to find clothing and food as well as raise funds to support other activities performed by the Santa Maria Chapter of the American Red Cross. She was awarded a Presidential Citation by Woodrow Wilson for her outstanding service.

Mary overcame many trials in her pioneering life. Her struggles were many but her fortitude greater. Whether it was a broken ankle from being thrown from a horse as a young mother, the burns she suffered escaping her ranch house fire with her children or an attack by a deranged young woman who stuck her in a rage leading to her eventual blindness, she bore up with patience and faith.

Mary wore contact lenses so that she could continue to attend church and clubs regularly. She wanted to live her life to its fullest measure. Her lenses wouldn't have been easy or comfortable for her to wear. The first contact lens was invented in 1887 by A.E. Fick, a Swiss physician. Made from blown glass, they were difficult to fit and covered the eye not just the cornea.

The first contact lenses were made from heavy blown glass and covered the whole eye.
Source: twitter.com/lensfactory/status/ 557316073742430208

> The significance of the flag's design is more commonly known than that of its colors. The color red is for courage and readiness to sacrifice, white for pure intentions and high ideals, and blue for vigilance and justice. Today, the 50 stars stand for the 50 united states, and the 13 red and white stripes represent the 13 original colonies that drew together to form our nation.

Mary bore her hardships in stride, never coddled, with a will to survive with grace and a smile. As she was want to explain to those she shared her life story with, "There was water to be pumped and carried in buckets, sickness miles from doctors, small children to be tended to, and farming, cooking and crops to be managed, all in a day's work."

Mary Winters' life, which had spanned from the beginning of the American Civil War, resulted in her growing up during reconstruction, facing the horrors of the Great War, suffering through the Depression, and watching the expansion of the continental United States and an ever-changing flag as it transitioned from 34 stars to 48. She witnessed the Stock Market Crash of 1929 and endured the Great Depression, heard via radio the attack on Pearl Harbor and persevered through to witness the end of World War II. What an era of historical events to have experienced in one lifetime! Through all of these events, she watched her country change from an agrarian society to using phones instead of telegraphs and automobiles instead of horses. She lived in extraordinary times.

Henrietta Louise Newlove Martin (1870-1921)

Henrietta and John Newlove wedding picture, November 1888
Source: Santa Maria Valley Historical Society collection.

Henrietta Louise Newlove was one of eleven children born to John and Maria Beynon Newlove. John was a native of Lincolnshire, England, and Maria was from Temperanceville, Ontario, Canada. John had arrived in Canada at age 14 working for wages on a farm until he met Maria Ann Beynon. Both of them finding the winters very severe in Canada, the young couple married and made the trip to California via ship traversing Panama by land.

Hattie, as she was fondly called, was born near Salinas on May 23, 1870. This was an amazing decade to be born into. The telephone by Alexander Graham Bell was introduced, followed by Thomas Edison's first version of the light bulb and the phonograph. In New York City, construction began on the Brooklyn Bridge. The Standard Oil Company was founded. The nation was a bursting with innovation and growth. The excitement was palpable.

By 1875, the Newloves were farming in the Oso Flaco precinct at San Luis Obispo with eight children. In 1881 the family moved to the Santa Maria Valley and settled on a ranch southeast of today's Orcutt. Hattie was an adventurous child. She loved riding horses. She would often help herd the cattle and enjoyed the chance to ride to Sisquoc, a half day away, to pick up the mail. Of course, all of this energy and outdoor nature lead to what she said was "a big mistake." She learned to milk cows and so that chore was often "offered" to her.

Hattie's father John was very dedicated to his religion and insisted his children make the ten-mile trip to Santa Maria to the Methodist church on Sundays, even if he couldn't attend. The ride made by horse and buggy was quite the undertaking, and the children made the most of the event. If the trek were made without parents, the children would send one sibling to church to hear the sermon, and the rest would go visit friends in town. On the way home the sermon was recounted by the one drafted to attend so that all of the children could answer their father's inquiries and thus keep the opportunities coming.

On November 14, 1888, Hattie was married to Robert Franklin Martin at the Newlove Ranch in a double-ring ceremony with her sister Sadie and Herbert W. Head. Frank was born in Santa Rosa, California, in 1866. In the Voter registration log circa 1892, Frank Martin is described as a farmer living in La Graciosa, light completion, blue eyes, brown hair, 5'10" tall.

Hattie and Frank would have eight children between 1890 and 1905. Four boys were born before their first daughter Pauline Nevada Martin arrived in 1898. Pauline remembers her mother as very outgoing and friendly. Whenever they rode into Santa Maria in their two-seat horse and buggy, Hattie seemingly stopped to talk to everyone. Pauline would tug at her mother's skirt trying to speed her along so that they could get to town and visit Coblentz and Schwabacher's for a handful of paper-wrapped candy. Hattie made sure to take a bag back to her other children.

Hattie's father John died in 1889, a year after her marriage to Frank. Much began happening during the short time after his passing. Her mother Maria, now a widow, was beset with offers to purchase the Newlove land, presumably for farming sheep. Maria had continued dry-farming and raising livestock just as before her husband's death. It was not an easy existence without a man to do the heavy lifting and deal with the business of the ranch. Maria continued to work the land for another five years. Finally, in 1904 with Hattie's encouragement, Maria decide to take a more informed look at what might be inspiring the persistence in the men who were approaching her with incrementally increasing offers. The whisperers and speculators were talking of oil, the value of which was pretty minimally understood until more and more automobiles took to roads all over the world and more and more manufacturing turned to internal combustion engines to crank out their products. Fortunately, Maria had retained the family land. An oil boom consumed the valley, and there was an explosion in her land's value! Great prosperity overtook the hard-working family as the ranch was sold to Union Oil Company for one million dollars. Rumors circulated, inflating the number to $3.5 million over the generations to follow. At the time the value of one million dollars in today's equivalent would be $26 million dollars. This kind of prosperity had been unimaginable!

Henrietta Louise Newlove Martin remains
Source: findagrave.com

Martin house at 800 South Broadway
Source: Santa Maria Valley Historical Society collection.

This fortune permitted many experiences, among them was a transcontinental train trip in a private rail car to her mother's ancestral home in Canada. In 1909, Hattie, her mother and her extended family had visited the Beynon Family experiencing what she called "a trip of a lifetime." Maria Ann Newlove died in 1913, and Hattie used her part of the inheritance to build a beautiful home at 800 S. Broadway. This location is across the street from the Santa Maria Inn. There is no other way to describe the home but a mansion.

Unfortunately, Hattie would be taken ill for several years, suffering much pain but with good humor, it was reported. A devout Methodist, despite the early antics of her childhood, Hattie passed away at age 51 on April 19, 1921, after a long illness kept her housebound for two years. She preceded her husband of 33 years and all eight of her children.

Chapter Four: Town Builders

Mary Antoinette McClain Blosser (1865-1958)

Mary Antoinette McClain Blosser
Source: ancestry.com

Mary was born September 13, 1865, to Joseph B. and Maria Georgia Fuente McClain in San Jose, Santa Clara County, California. Her parents were born in Chile, although it appears they spent most of their adult lives in California. Early records of her life were destroyed by fire. At an interview in 1953, she didn't remember much preceding her arrival with her family in the sleepy town of Central City. She arrived with her parents, as a little girl, with a four-horse team pulling all their worldly belongings. The town, as she recalled, was one store and one blacksmith shop located at Broadway and Main Street.

Mary attended first grade at Pleasant Valley School. Joseph McClain was a farmer in Betteravia when Laguna Lake was in existence there. She was 17 years old when Central City became Santa Maria in 1882.

Mary and Garrett Blosser married in 1893 when Mary was 27 years old. The U.S. in the 1800s, with land and resources plentiful, found most 19th-century couples married at an early age. Between 1800 and 1900, women generally married for the first time between the ages of 20 and 22. Most of the young ladies in the Valley married in their teens, so 27 was definitely an "advanced age." Perhaps Mary was waiting on just the right man.

> The only hanging in the little town, in the year 1890, happened at the 76 Saloon. A vigilante committee executed a saloon keeper, Edmund Luther Criswell. Criswell shot and killed Constable I. W. Southard in an exchange of gunfire. May 9th of that year, a number of masked men entered the saloon where Criswell was being held before trial, disarming the guards. Criswell's feet and hands were bound, a rope was thrown over a rafter, and Criswell was hung for a murderer in his own saloon without due process.
>
> This event was the talk of the town. An almost unimaginable action by a town that was known to be very law and order in its demeanor. However, Criswell had tried the valley's patience with his disregard for decency and the law. It was proven that he was a man of desperate character. He had murdered a man back east before coming to the valley. He had spent some years in jail, was suspected of deserting the Union Army during the American Civil War, and had tried to murder his own son in Los Alamos. He additionally threatened three or four of the city's prominent citizens with destruction of their businesses (arson). The murder of the constable was the last straw and Criswell's last act of terrorism on a town.
>
> While the vigilantes acted with righteous vengeance and no one was saddened to see Criswell meet his maker, the town was troubled and mortified by the hanging. In the end it was universally condemned and a jury convened to officially chronicle and declare the action illegal. Criswell's grave is unmarked to this day. He was universally considered so reprehensible, it was feared his final resting place might be desecrated, his body disinterred.

Maybe a late bloomer, Mary lived to be 92 years old and, as a Santa Maria Valley pioneer, she was often interviewed about her memories and experiences. A jovial, good natured person, Mary shared many memories about the growing up of a village to a town. Since Mary experienced Santa Maria

Chapter Four: Town Builders

with only hundreds of residents to approaching 20,000 before her last days, she had a lot to share—after all, her husband was Garrett L. Blosser, marshal the year Santa Maria was first incorporated as a city. He served as a deputy sheriff and constable for 42 years. Maria's pillow talk would most likely have been of all the skeletons hidden her husband's long career!

Mary witnessed the growth and history of our valley over her 92 years. Married to the main law enforcement officer in our valley, dinner conversation was probably very interesting. However, her fondest memories were of her husband himself, and she kept a photograph near her even though he had been gone more than 40 years when she passed away in 1958. Mary had witnessed firsthand, in her lifetime, Reconstruction through World Wars I and II and the early days of the Viet Nam Conflict. She had experienced the birth and growing pains of our town from its vigilante roots to law and order.

Mary Blosser and her children Ernest and Mabel.
Source: Santa Maria Valley Historical Society collection.

Eleonore Begou Renoult Roemer (1865-1939)

Eleonore Begou Renoult Roemer
Source: Santa Maria Valley Historical Society collection.

Eleonore was Mrs. Joseph Roemer when she arrived in Santa Maria. Joseph Roemer was her second husband. First married to Japhet Frances Renoult in April 11, 1885, Eleonore was widowed with two small children on January 12, 1892, in Riverside, California, at the age of 27.

Her life with Frank Renoult was one of travel. Born in Strasbourg, Bas-Rhin, Alsace, France, she immigrated in 1885. Eleonore Begou and Frank Renoult married when she was twenty years old. Frank, an artist, is listed in many places as a pictorial painter. Born in San Francisco around 1853, his work must have forced him to change locations frequently as he was in Denver, Colorado, in 1874, San Luis Obispo in 1875, Los Angeles in 1886, San Bernardino in 1887 and Riverside in 1888.

Eleonore and Frank had two children in Riverside, California: a son Alfred Frances born in 1888 and a daughter Jessie Alma born in October, 1890. Frank's passing in January of 1892 left Eleonore with two small children to care for and no resources to do it.

Eleonore married 57-year-old divorcee Joseph Roemer of Santa Maria four months later in April of 1892. She was 27 years old. Joseph adopted young Alfred, and Jessie assumed the Roemer name. A son, Frank Lloyd, was born to the couple in March of 1893.

Joseph Roemer, a blacksmith by trade, was more artisan than artist. He often invented tools for his trade. A wrench of his own design was patented and in use as late as the 1950s. Unfortunately, trusting the wrong people led to the theft of the patent, and he never saw a cent on his invention. Joseph Roemer was no stranger to twists of fate.

He was born aboard ship in New York's harbor while his parents were quarantined awaiting release to America. His father was sent ashore for food but became engaged in a street fight and was killed. This unfortunate and ill-timed event forced Mrs. Roemer to return to her native Austria-Hungary with the newborn Joseph. Mrs. Roemer would have had only a glimpse of a future in America. She undoubtedly shared her dreams in stories with her son, growing in him a longing to live in the land of his birth. Joseph, age 25, would finally manage to return in 1860 during a time of great political unrest. When he arrived, he didn't hang around for the bloody battles of the American Civil War, he headed west.

Eleonore and Joseph must have seemed an unusual couple in those first days after her arrival in the Valley with her two small children having married a divorced and much older husband. No one is quite sure how they came to be together although some family descendants seem to think that their sisters introduced the idea of a match between them, and Joseph went to Riverside to make the marriage. Whatever brought them together, they were seemingly very devoted to one another, and there was great trust. Her name often appeared as partner or officer on the businesses. The Roemer companies and investments that Joseph began were handed down to sons Alfred and Frank. Jessie would marry and leave the area, but her only child, a son, although he failed to thrive and live to adulthood, had born the first name Roemer.

Descendants of Joseph and Eleonore would be in business in Santa Maria selling farm supplies into the 21st century.

Roemer Hardware, N. Broadway.
Source: Santa Maria Valley Historical Society collection.

Married 37 years, Joseph lived to 92 years of age leaving Eleonore widowed again in 1929. Her last day would be in February of 1939 at age 73 this time surrounded with a sense of a life well lived.

Sarah Jane Dayment Smith (1844-1938)

Sarah Jane Dayment Smith
Source: Santa Maria Valley Historical Society collection.

Sarah and William Smith were English pioneers who traveled through Canada to reach the United States. William Smith, born in Yorkshire England, immigrated to eastern Canada in 1849 where he met Sarah Jane, 11 years his junior. She had arrived in Canada from Devonshire, England. They had both been attracted by tales of gold and silver in the West. They married and followed a dream that had captured their imaginations. They left eastern Canada by boat with all of their worldly possessions, including a piano.

Surviving the many challenges of crossing via the Isthmus of Panama, the Smiths were treated to quite the view as they neared the coast of California, the Golden Gate, a narrow entrance between the Pacific Ocean and the San Francisco Bay. The strait was named by explorer and U.S. Army officer John C. Frémont, who marveled at its beauty in 1846.

However, the awe of the view was obliterated as the ship on which they were entering the strait began to list dangerously and eventually caught fire. All cargo was lost, including the piano that had survived the isthmus crossing. Passengers were rushed to the lifeboats. Most passengers were soldiers as they were arriving in the last days of the American Civil War. Sarah, clutching her infant son, Frank, leaped overboard into the arms of a man in one of the small life boats. She and her baby son were unharmed, but her relief and happiness was soon eclipsed by the knowledge that all of the fine household linens, clothing and prized personal possessions, so carefully packed and selected to travel, were lost.

Arriving dry, now afloat in the small life boat paddled by soldiers and crew but without any goods to their name, the Smiths pushed on with a much lighter load to Virginia City, Nevada. Virginia City sprang up as a boomtown with the 1859 discovery of the Comstock Lode, the first major silver deposit discovery in the United States. Silver and gold were buried deep beneath her streets, and both men and women traveled from around the world to live and work. Miners pulled millions of dollars from shafts and tunnels 3,000 feet beneath the thriving town where, at its peak of population in the mid-1870s, it had an estimated

> The voyage, with only a brief land crossing at the Isthmus of Panama, was 5,850 miles, New York to San Francisco. Adding an additional few days and miles to get from eastern Canada to New York, hoping for a very brief layover in Panama, the entire trek could not have been completed in less than 45 days. This would also assume that weather was good both at sea and on land. Panama often challenged travelers with cholera, yellow fever, malaria and dysentery if they were held up waiting for a westbound ship for very long. There were few ships to California. Many people were stuck in Panama City for weeks, if not months. The pathway across Panama was jungle, 75 miles up the Chagres River, then 25 miles by mule to Panama City. Those miles were not uneventful either. Snakes, of water and land variety, awaited any misstep. Eventually, a Panama railway was built to make traversing the east-west crossing somewhat more comfortable (for nothing could make the weather more bearable!), but the Smiths arrived before this luxury and crossed with a wagon and the piano!

Chapter Four: Town Builders

25,000 residents who worked, lived, worshiped, educated and died pursuing the dream of vast and immediate wealth.

Their second son, Charles William, was born in September of 1868 in Virginia City. The next year, Sarah must have had her fill of the wild and raucous place as she began encouraging Mr. Smith to move the family. Like many before them, silver and gold brought them west, but it would be the land that would capture them for a lifetime.

The Smiths moved on to Arroyo Grande, where they began operated an inn, stage line and post office for the next two years. In 1871, they arrived in Central City. Acquiring land, the Smith's made a generous contribution of one acre on which the Pleasant Valley School was built by R.D. Cook. Mr. Smith engaged in farming and did so until his passing in 1901.

Sarah had eight children during her lifetime. The one most associated with the valley was Charles William. Charles was heavily involved in Santa Maria's early days, and his family led a good life. In addition to raising horses of great reputation, he set up a grain mart and real estate agency. He later served as city councilman and deputy county assessor. He was married to Myrtle Hudson and they had three sons: William Leland, Charles Douglas and Marian Augustus Smith. The three of them were quite standouts in their fields: Leland as a dentist in Santa Maria and Douglas and Marian as Superior Court of Santa Barbara County judges. The original Santa Maria Smith home still stands today, although it has been moved to a new location, awaits restoration and was subsequently owned by the Enos Family.

Sarah Jane Smith died in 1938 at the age of 94. She had arrived in the Santa Maria Valley in 1871 and was well known among the early pioneers of the valley even though her last days were spent in San Diego after 1912. She was making her home with two of her daughters and her oldest son Frank Smith (the baby she jumped ship with) when she passed.

The Smith family: Sarah and William and children Frank, Charles, Frederick, Walter, Arthur, Minnie, Nettie and Albert.
Source: Santa Maria Valley Historical Society collection.

Chapter Four: Town Builders

Elizabeth Mary Oakley May (1895-1981)

Elizabeth Oakley May
Source: Santa Maria Valley Historical Society collection.

The town was building momentum. A generation had been born and, in turn, watched the valley establish itself as a true sweet spot in California. The table is set for those originals to raise children to populate our valley. Elizabeth Oakley is a daughter of this valley. She is born on a 3,000-acre family ranch on the Alamo Creek in August of 1895 to William C. and Bertha Belle Rice Oakley.

The Oakley girls, c. 1912, left-to-right: Lois, Helen, Marion, Elizabeth and Isabelle.
Source: Santa Maria Valley Historical Society collection.

Beth, as she will be known, is something of a historian and writer sharing details of her life from her earliest recollections. Her upbringing in this proud pioneering family is quite discernable as she regales generations with details of Oakley valley life. "We were almost self-sufficient, having our own orchard and vegetable garden. Mother made jams and jellies," she would recall vividly. "Together, we canned 200 or more pounds of peaches and apricots annually, as well as pears, berries and quinces. Father made hominy from our corn. We raised our own ham, bacon, sausage and lard, as well as milk, cream, butter, and cottage cheese. Chickens, turkeys and ducks were also raised on the ranch. Bills were paid twice a year, in the spring when the cattle were sold and then again in the fall after threshing."

Beth's grandparents, John and Nancy Whaley, are buried in the Santa Maria Cemetery. They came to California in 1850 with 11 children. A daughter, Elizabeth Whaley, married Cary Calvin Oakley who had come to the state alone from Tennessee. Beth's father was known as Will Oakley. He and Bertha Belle Rice, sometimes called Birdie, lived on the ranch on the Alamo until 1902 when they moved to town for their children to attend school. Beth was seven years old at the time. She would attend high school in 1910 and then on to San Francisco Normal, a vocational trade school: a "normal school," whose primary mission was to train young ladies for the profession of teaching. She graduated in 1914 with a Bachelor of Arts from the University of Southern California in Los Angeles.

Chapter Four: Town Builders

Between 1900-1918, Beth was with her parents at 323 Mill Street. Beth Oakley married Fred May in 1917. Fred too came from family rich in Valley history. Before their marriage, Fred entered the Great War and served as an army First Sergeant. This must have taken Beth's breath away as the horrific stories of war were already reaching the Santa Maria Times. After Fred returned from the Great War and they married, they lived at 913 S. McClelland.

Beside the war other troubles were a-brewing locally. Whiskey Row was a black mark on Santa Maria's downtown progression and prosperity. While Beth May was quite the refined lady, it is her memories of Santa Maria along "Whiskey Row," that gives us the greatest insight into her sense of humor.

One morning, Beth Oakley and her sisters listened through closed doors to a whispered conversation between their parents. There had been a raid. One of the houses on Mill Street had been stormed the night before. Her father, Will Oakley, a member of "The Good Government League" had joined in breaking down the door. As fate would have it, one of the patrons of the establishment that night was "a pillar of the community." Stricken with panic, he called out that he would be ruined.

> From the first moments of Central City, there was a battle forming between the "drys and the wets." Most of the saloons were located in the 100 block on the north side of Main street, the strip known as Whiskey Row. Rows of houses of ill-repute lined the south side of Mill Street, just two blocks north of Whiskey Row. Church people, members of the Women's Temperance Union and the Improvement Club, tried in vain to rid the town of this "taint." The dank and dingy jailhouse at the end of the block was no deterrent to the corruption and practices of Whiskey Row.
>
> Word was that husbands and fathers forbid their lady folks to walk along East Mill Street. Perhaps because they didn't want to be spotted in any of the myriad of businesses associated with Whiskey Row! Ladies told of crossing to the south side of Main Street to avoid too close of contact with the commotion that was Whiskey Row. Yet years have a way of drawing some rather interesting confessions from the prim matrons and ingénues from sheltered homes of that era. The painted and powdered ladies from the district did catch the eye and inspire some envy with their flashy dress, crimped hair in high pompadours and huge hats. Riding about town in horse-drawn buggies, many were seen at the race track on East Main Street. Local girls were curious, not so much about the activity of Whiskey Row as the fashions!

Oakley went on to share with his wife that a sympathetic pal whispered, "Turn around and pretend you are one of us!" Perhaps it was this kind of half-hearted enforcement that kept Whiskey Row such a fixture in town for multiple generations. The gentleman in question saved his reputation with quick action and quiet collaborators!

From before the Great Depression through World War II, Beth Oakley May registered as a democrat and a teacher. She spent her career in the public school system. Beth taught school at Mill Street, Bonita and Orcutt elementary schools until retirement. She served 34 years on the City Library Board and was president of the Pioneer Association in 1967. Her father, Will Oakley, was a founding member of the Pioneer Association and hosted the first gathering in 1923, which with certainty Beth attended.

On February 19, 1942, President Franklin D. Roosevelt signed Executive Order 9066, which called for the internment of all Japanese Americans from the West Coast. In the Santa Maria Valley, the busses loaded up the Japanese population in Guadalupe. They were divested of most of their belongings, allowed only two small suitcases or bags of belongings. Beth May wrote letters to the families of her students at the Tulare Assembly Center. She apologized for the hardship, sent coloring books, home news and well wishes. They wrote her back, thanking her for her kind words

Chapter Four: Town Builders

of support. All looked forward to the end of the war so that everyone could return home and resume their lives as before. Much was shared in the correspondence: hope, love and faith for a future filled with all good things. Beth May obviously felt great compassion for her Japanese-American neighbors. She stood with them through the hardship.

Letters sent to Elizabeth May from Japanese students interned with their parents during the Second World War
Source: Santa Maria Valley Historical Society collection.

Beth's years spanned an enormous amount of American history. Born in one century, she flourished in another. A pioneer daughter of the Valley, born at the end of the 19th century, descended from pre-Revolutionary War immigrants, Beth witnessed major wars, economic disasters, and ultimately great prosperity. She started astride horses and in wagons and finished with the automobile and flight. While she might not have seen the end of the detested Whiskey Row, she did vote and enjoy the fruits of much social innovation. Beth died at age 86. She and Fred had one son, Fred O. May.

Chapter Five: Splitting Centuries

The Women's Rights Movement names July 13, 1848, as its beginning, although it sometimes seems every generation of women believes they are starting the liberation movement. In part this belief is sustained because there is always so much left to be achieved with each passing generation. In upstate New York on that particular July date, it was a sweltering summer day. The heat, probably contributed to the ill temperament of a young housewife and mother named Elizabeth Cady Stanton. She was invited to afternoon tea with four of her women friends. It would seem that it is always tea that starts a revolution! When the course of their conversation turned from the blistering heat to the current status of women in society, Stanton poured out her extreme displeasure surrounding the social injustices suffered by women. The American Revolution had been fought 70 years earlier to win the American patriots freedom from tyranny. "Are women not patriots?" she would rail. Her query was why had women not gained the same freedom as the men? Both had equally experienced the immense risks through those perilous war years. America, this new republic, would surely benefit from having women play active roles throughout society much as they had done throughout the revolution. This was not the first small group of women to have such a conversation, and it definitely was not the last.

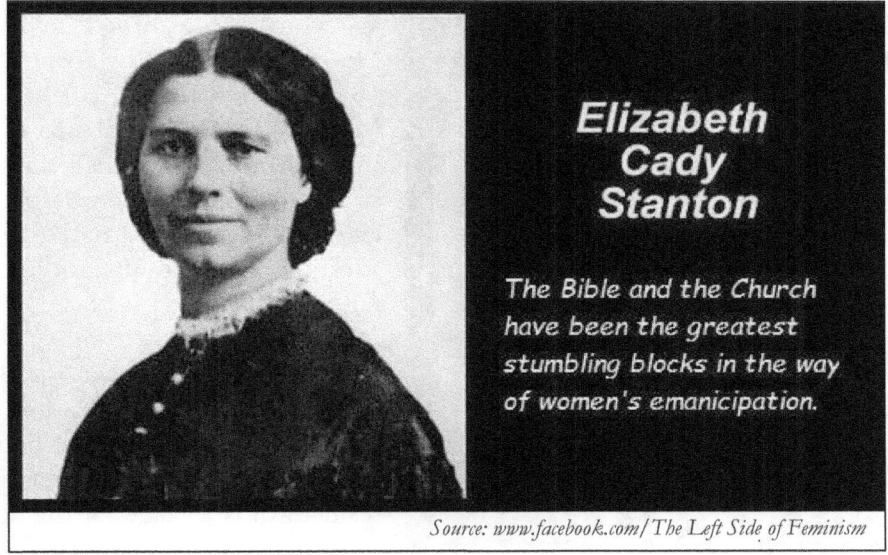

Source: www.facebook.com/The Left Side of Feminism

Elizabeth Cady Stanton

The Bible and the Church have been the greatest stumbling blocks in the way of women's emanicipation.

Sarah Frances Harris Lewis (1858-1951)

Sarah Frances Harris Lewis
Source: Santa Maria Valley Historical Society collection.

Sarah Frances Harris' lifetime straddled two centuries. She was at the forefront of the interval that brought the new age woman to maturity. Sarah was the daughter of Mr. and Mrs. James Handy Harris. She was born December 3, 1858. Her father had sailed through the Straights of Magellan from his Alabama in 1849 pursuing wealth during the California Gold Rush era. He had had the same fortune as the majority of men before him, no vast golden destiny awaited him. He did find a wife in the community of Mark West, Sonoma County, California, start a family and build a farm.

Sarah's family arrived in the Santa Maria area when it was nothing more than a treeless plain rife with wild animals and no visible water. Their first night, the family camped on the Nipomo mesa. Sarah was nine years old and would be a resident of the valley for the next 83 years.

The first five years, Sarah would recall, could only be described as "terrible." Most families were absolutely destitute as crops failed and grasshoppers plagued the area three years in a row. She went on to share, "During the worst of it, the skies were darkened for three days with the pests." Even getting an education was difficult; fortunately, Sarah was privately tutored by her Uncle Joel Miller. He charged $2 a month but only held school for three months of the year.

Carving a life, building a town, getting an education in a near empty wilderness was formidable. To say that most families were "scratching out" an existence wasn't an understatement. For Sarah and the other girls growing up here gave them the fortitude to make changes, to better their situations.

Charles A. Lewis had been but a visitor to Central City in the mid-1870s. He came to visit an aunt and help out; he stayed for Sarah "Sadie" Harris. It's hard to say when Sarah started being known as Sadie, but on October 5, 1876, she became Mrs. Charles Lewis. They were married by the Justice of the Peace, Madison Thornburgh, in Central City. Santa Maria had not yet been named.

Charlie was a farmer, like most of the residents of Central City, but during the early 1880s Sadie worked as a cook in a hotel. She also took in washing for various clientele. One of her customers was a man known as "Tambo."

Tambo's real name was Michael Mullee. He was small and pug-faced with a red mustache so long he could almost tie it under his chin. He ran his own saloon and "hotel" catering to the lowest class of patrons. Although a generally jovial fellow, he was the source of problems in town. Drunken brawls and physical violence became common place at his groggery. It wasn't long until even Tambo could see the writing on the wall. Knowing he was in trouble with the local residents, he told Sadie that if he were to be run out of town, he would deed his property to her.

When Tambo was confronted by a group of vigilantes and given 48 hours to vacate, he notified Sadie and prepared himself. At the end of the 48 hours, he showed up before the group with a constable in tow to protect himself. However, the angry group discharged the constable pointing out that he was outside his jurisdiction. A bonfire was lighted at the intersection of Main and Broadway. Tambo must have expected to be hanged, but upon concluding that the plan was to tar and feather him and ride him out of town, he was actually cheered-up in spirit. Hard to believe, but this was good news! It was just past midnight on October 13, 1882, when Tambo left town. Sadie recalled, "I delivered washing to him. He paid me, then advised me to take possession of his property. I promptly moved into his house. There were those that tried to take it away from me, but I had possession and he had filed a deed in San Luis Obispo transferring it to me, so I kept it!"

The Lucas sanitarium, located at 724 South Broadway was torn down to make room for Lyons Restaurant.
Source: Santa Maria Valley Historical Society collection.

When Union Sugar Company began operations in 1897, Sadie took charge of the kitchen in the hotel, working as a cook for a number of years. In 1900 when Sadie was 42, her husband Charlie's health, never dependable, was so poor that he decided to go to Nevada and find "a cure."

The turn of the century brought with it a new career for Sadie. She became one of the earliest practical nurses in Santa Maria. She worked with her uncle, Dr. J.S. Miller, as well as with Dr. Thomas Lucas. She would continue for more than 50 years at this profession.

Sadie wasn't a young woman when she came to work in medicine, but she was motivated. Her son Claude had been tragically killed at age 15 in 1895 when a wagon ran over him. The loss and her inability to aid him deeply imprinted on her heart. Five years later her husband passed at age 49.

Sadie Lewis was a part of the developing "new breed" of woman. She worked outside the home and was socially active in her community. Always energetic, she was associated with the Christian Church having been baptized in the mud of Nipomo Creek. She was also an active member of Native Daughters of the Golden West. The Native Daughters is a fraternal and patriotic organization founded on the principles of: love of home, devotion to the flag, veneration of the pioneers and faith in the existence of God.

Sadie Lewis' obituary would remind the town she had been the oldest living woman in Santa Maria when she celebrated her 90th birthday in 1948. In an article the *Santa Maria Times* asked her to what she attributed her longevity. "I have never smoked and never drank. I don't know what a cigarette or liquor tastes like and don't want to know." Sarah Frances Harris Lewis passed away at her daughter Estelle Hick's house on East Church in April 1951.

Minna "Minnie" Allott Stearns (1863-1948)

Minnie Allott Stearns
Source: Santa Maria Valley Historical Society collection.

Mrs. Minnie A. Stearns arrived in the Santa Maria Valley in the fall of 1893. She was accompanied by her two young sons, Raymond and Burt. Her parents Joseph and Tamar Eliza Allott were living in Santa Maria. She and her children decided to be near family and had come to live on a ranch with her sister and brother-in-law, Charles Curryer.

Minnie Allott arrived in the United States in 1868 from England with her parents and her brother Harry. She received some formal art training in Wilmington, Delaware, around 1887. Minnie came to California for unspecified health reasons. She worked as a court reporter in Los Angeles for a time. It was there in the summer of 1888 that she met and married Charles W. Stearns, originally from Wisconsin.

After their marriage, Charles became ill, and it became necessary for Minnie to go to work and support the family. She found employment in a packing house in Redland, California.

Minnie came to the Santa Maria Valley with her sons most probably because she had family connections through Harriet Sharp Hart. Soon after coming to the Valley, Minnie started a painting class which was attended by women of the town. She taught oil painting, mostly landscapes and china painting or porcelain painting; the decoration of glazed porcelain objects such as plates, bowls, vases or statues. Her studio was originally in Lucas Hall at 211 West Main; she lived above on the second floor. Her son Raymond became the janitor for Lucas Hall.

It's unclear what was wrong with Charles Stearns, but he passed away in 1898 in a California State Hospital in Los Angeles five years after Minnie arrived in the Santa Maria Valley. State hospitals in California at this time were usually reserved for the mentally compromised or inebriates. Whatever his situation, it could not have been easy for Minnie to take her sons and leave him behind.

Santa Maria, from its beginning, supported education, art and culture. Mrs. Stearns was a welcomed addition in the valley. She became the first art and music teacher in the high school in 1904 and taught through 1908. In 1908 she accepted the position as librarian in the Carnegie Public Library where she remained until she retired in 1934 after 25 years.

The Carnegie Library in Santa Maria was attained through the dedication and diligent work of the Ladies Literary Society, known today as the Minerva Club. The idea of a library began in 1894 when 25 women, wanting to expand not only their knowledge but that of their children decided to pursue the idea of a public library. This inspiration would take years to bring to fruition. James F.

Chapter Five: Splitting Centuries

Goodwin would provide the opening donation that eventually lead to meeting Andrew Carnegie's requirements for the funding of a public library. Construction began in August of 1908 when city treasurer William A. Haslam announced the contractor with the winning bid.

Minnie began her career at the library at a salary of $70 per month. She was both librarian and janitor. She would have the same wages until 1924, when the city council would raise her to $110.

In 1910 Minnie's family was virtually under one roof at 615 S. Lincoln Street in Santa Maria. Both her parents, her brother Harry and her youngest son Burt were living and working locally. Minnie at the Carnegie Library, her father Joseph as a gardener and her brother as a machinist at a local garage.

Carnegie Library
Source: Santa Maria Valley Historical Society collection.

After her parents passing in the 1920s, she took in lodgers at her Lincoln address for many years, usually teachers at the high school. Emma R. McKenzie (previously Emma Childs) a high school teacher and Elizabeth L. Smith, a domestic arts teacher, both lived with her for several years.

Not much is known about Minnie over the next few years. Her son Burt died in 1929 at the age of 36 leaving her three granddaughters. When she passes in 1948, her son Raymond was still alive and living at her Lincoln Street address with his wife Clarita.

Minnie A. Stearns died in San Luis Obispo, 12 October 1948, at the age of 86. She was well remembered as the first librarian in Santa Maria.

Chapter Five: Splitting Centuries

Ida May Twitchell Blochman (1854-1931)

Ida May Twitchell Blochman
Source: Santa Maria Valley Historical Society collection.

Ida was born in Bangor, Penobscot County, Maine, April 11, 1854. In 1860, she was living with her family in Iowa: father, Martin Carr Twitchell; mother, Lucy Howard; a sister, Mary; and her brother, Fremont. Her father registered for the draft during the American Civil War, but with a family and age 41, he wasn't called up. They were still residing together in 1870.

Some unknown family upheaval must have occurred between the census of 1870, when she was 16, and her arrival in the Valley. She came to the small community of La Graciosa in 1879 to join her mother, Lucy, and her brother, Fremont, who had settled on acreage on Orcutt Road. Although her father would come to the area and is buried in the Santa Maria Cemetery, it is unclear what his relationship to Lucy Howard Twitchell was after 1870.

Ida's father had several professions, one of them was teacher. She seemed to have inherited his passion for education. She was a graduate of the State University at Ames, Iowa, before attending the Teachers Institute in Lompoc. She was principal of the Santa Maria Grammar School for six years. Ida was of the mind that our very reason for being was to teach the next generation to be better than we are.

Ida had found teaching to be very fulfilling. She spent all her time teaching, preparing to teach and at other scholarly tasks. She held that there was no time for frivolities, but she was not a stern person, rather noted for sweetness and endless patience with her students. She was more a no "frills" kind of personality. Her clothes were black and white: white shirtwaists and black skirts, no jewelry except for a pin and later her wedding ring. Her shoes were plain black oxfords. Her hair was worn in soft waves, drawn back from a center part and coiled into a knot at the back of her head. She wore rimless glasses which she often removed, her eyes twinkling as she challenged a student with an idea or a question.

Ida was a happy soul, very content, always learning and sharing. She had a wonderful sense of humor and was great company for family, students and colleagues. In the mid-1880s, she lived in a two-story frame house with the Thornburghs: Minerva and John, a family known for enjoying company and who often invited visitors and guests to their parlor to read aloud and enjoy poetry. It was a wonderful and loving setting for Ida, who also had the company of another teacher at the house, Emma Childs.

In the spring of 1882, a gentleman came to Santa Maria of almost the opposite ilk. Lazar E. Blochman, of San Francisco, was restless and unhappy at his work. He kept a diary, and on his arrival, he remarked, "…Santa Maria is a hamlet of less than 500 inhabitants, with no paved streets, no gardens, and no social life such as I have enjoyed before." Blochman was a cousin of the

Chapter Five: Splitting Centuries

Kaisers, for whom he first worked, and, when they sold to Weilheimer and Coblentz, he became an employee of that firm. He felt lonely and dismal about his future until he met Ida Twitchell.

Blochman and a friend named McKenzie, who was the local station agent, came to call on the two young and very witty teachers staying at the Thornburg's. In 1888, both couples married and became lifelong friends.

Blochman and Ida were a very good match. He was an intellectual with a lively mind, and she brought out of him an ebullient spirit. Inspired by James F. Goodwin's tree project, he became so enthusiastic about tree and fruit culture that he bought acreage for experimentation. Goodwin hated the lack of trees in the valley scenery and recognized the good things that trees could provide. Blochman became well involved with Goodwin, who had also inspired William Laird Adam and Samuel Jefferson Jones to support development of trees in the valley. As a civic gesture, Blochman planted trees to add to the beauty of the growing town. Ida and Lazar lived in a small house on East Cook Street after their marriage; then he built a home at 801 S. Broadway for them as he was quite an accomplished architect too. It was here that the they planted gardens, ornamental shrubs, gum and cypress trees. Ida herself loved botany; she collected, classified and pressed wildflowers. Some of her collection were part of the County exhibit at the Chicago World Fair Exposition in 1893.

Ida began teaching botany and wrote many essays for publication. After her marriage, she also became an excellent cook. Each year she canned fruit and made jellies and jams. These were also part of the exhibition at the exposition and were displayed in specially shaped glasses.

On October 5, 1894, Mrs. L. E. Blochman, Ida, was elected the first president of the Ladies Literary Society. This tiny pioneer town with changing names, possessed high ideals and a desire for ever greater prosperity in both mind and body. Currently populated by 1,200 residents and finally named Santa Maria, the ladies club formed with 25 original members and a mission to: "pursue intellectual, moral and spiritual values."

Ida was a dedicated educator, in 1889 at the Teacher's Institute of Los Angles, she read a paper on "Narcotics." In a later interview with the *Evening Express*, she expounded on the twin

Ida May Twichell Blochman
Source: Santa Maria Valley Historical Society collection.

evils of alcohol and tobacco. She advocated that instruction should be given in schools addressing the evil effects of both. She wanted her students to learn more than rote knowledge. She wanted them to acquire insight, and to make queries, on many social subjects. Mostly, she taught them how to study. She was quoted years later by students, "We must concentrate to learn." Her message to them succinctly put, "think."

Chapter Five: Splitting Centuries

Ida Blochman, Vice Principal, back row, 4th from the left
Source: Santa Maria Valley Historical Society collection.

In 1896, Ida began teaching in high school, as well as serving as vice principal. She dedicated herself to ensuring that Santa Maria Union High School became a four-year accredited institution.

The Blochman's had a very full and thriving life; they were well loved and respected in the valley. They discovered, however, that they could not have children of their own, so they adopted a little boy, Harry Ecklind Blochman.

Four years later, on July 3, 1901, 13-year-old Harry went missing. Last seen crossing a field to join some other neighbor boys to play, he failed to return home at the end of the day. The town was filling with Fourth of July revelers and families who had turned out for the usual pioneer fanfare that was common to Santa Maria. There was to be a parade on South Broadway and, with Harry's home immediately on the parade route, many of his friends showed up to knock on the door and inquire for his company on the 4th before the parade.

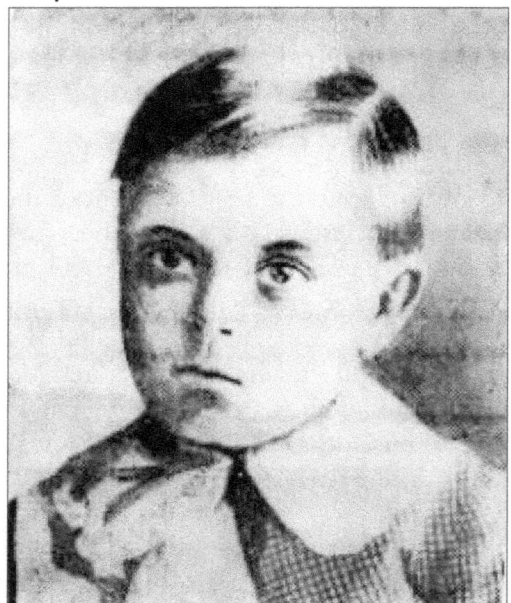

Harry Blochman photo published shortly after his murder on July 3, 1901.
Santa Maria Valley Historical Society collection.

It is hard to know what the Blochmans might have feared, but the worst came. Harry Blochman had been murdered, his body finally found with multiple stab wounds. Years would go by without any answers. Over the years, stories would arise as to who had murdered their child. There was even a prison death bed confession to the murder, but all of these revelations were many years away from the traumatic event. A year after Harry's death, the Blochman's adopted another boy, Leo.

Chapter Five: Splitting Centuries

In 1909, oil discovered on Blochman land, where much of the horticultural learning that had early on possessed Blochman, made them millionaires. The need to work and live in a small town disappeared overnight. Deciding to continue a life of scholarly pursuits, they sold their holdings at 801 S. Broadway to a Mr. McCoy who would build the Santa Maria Inn at that location, the rest to the oil companies. They moved to Berkeley, and L. E. Blochman, who had been an architect and a teacher without attending college, became a freshman at the age of 59. Ida continued to pursue cultural opportunities including the women's suffrage movement. She died in 1931, at age 77 in Berkeley, California.

Lucretia Hazel Reynolds Smith (1875-1936)

Lucretia was born in Canada on July 5, 1875, to Daniel and Mary Ann Reynolds. She immigrated with her family in 1876 to California. Three children were born to the Reynolds: George, Lucretia and Nancy. In 1880 the children were eight, five and three and living in Napa County, California. Lucretia's father traveled frequently for his health. He had built a beautiful home for his family on Telegraph Avenue in Oakland and, despite his frequent travels, the family maintained the location as the family home for many years. In 1874, Daniel Reynolds died leaving a widow and three small children.

The burden of his death caused financial reverses for the family, and Mrs. Reynolds found it necessary to go to work. She was a talented musician and turned her appreciable skill to the purpose of supporting her children. Her father's death at age 39 lead Lucretia, at age 10, to understand that life meant hard work, not play.

Lucretia supplemented a grammar school education with a business course and started out on her own at an early age. Four years of work experience on a country newspaper, the *St. Helena Star*, published in St. Helena,

Lucretia Hazel Reynolds Smith
Source: Santa Maria Valley Historical Society collection.

California, prepared Lucretia to seek a position in a large publishing house in San Francisco. She was well qualified and was able to advance rapidly. Within her first year she was retained as a special writer on the San Francisco dailies. Women were working as journalists, but they had to carefully guard themselves from being persuaded down paths men would never take. The term "gutter journalism," more recently referred to as gossip column surfaced, and Lucretia skirted away from any kind of entanglement in sensational styled journalism, especially concerning the private lives of public figures. She well understood the power of the reporter and the ability of the fourth estate to persuade people to either positive or negative perspectives on any topic. She held her responsibility to a higher standard sometimes realizing a much smaller pay packet in avoidance of questionable assignments. She felt the struggle was worth the suffering of a few smaller meals to maintain her integrity as a professional, serious journalist. To supplement her income, she wrote extensively publishing biographical sketches and some successful short stories.

In 1901, Lucretia married George Clinton Smith. Smith had been born in Ohio and moved first to Illinois, where he remained until 1874. At age 25, Smith moved to the Santa Maria Valley by covered wagon arriving in town when there were only six houses and the hills were filled with migrating geese. He was an industrious man with a mind for business. He tried his hand at farming then purchased an interest in the T.A. Jones Company. Smith was always moving his business venture ahead. With every profit, he reinvested again and usually bigger and with more at risk.

Chapter Five: Splitting Centuries

Smith decided to revisit his Midwest roots but soon returned to Santa Maria in 1882 and became manager of The Schwartz and BeeBee Lumberyard. He oversaw their interests as the Pacific Coast Railway was built in Santa Maria. He maintained the position for eight years while also pursuing his interest in real estate and as a grain buyer. Smith partnered with Daniel and George Curryer to purchase 80 acres of land south west of Santa Maria. They laid it out in parcels and put it on the market as town lots. This tract became known as the Smith and Curryer Addition. Smith planted many ornament trees by hand himself. He was a naturalist and enjoyed the value added of trees and flowers to the tracts.

Smith spent four years in San Francisco. It was during this time he met Lulu. On his return to Santa Maria with his talented young wife at his side, he again devoted his time to brokerage. After oil was discovered he turned his laudable sales talents to brokering oil. By 1907, his daily transactions totaled around $46,000.

Lucretia was much younger than George. He was 26 years her senior, but he was industrious and successful. After marriage, Lucretia still wrote and published biographies but she mostly took up charitable and temperance work. She joined the Improvement Club, where she held offices and worked relentlessly for its cause. She also hosted lectures in her home for advanced thought and started the Forensic Club, which promoted public speaking skills for "reasoned discourse in public life." Everyone was made welcome. Lucretia was a strong advocate for women, her mother's early struggles never far from her mind. She held strong opinions on how woman should be seen, treated and accepted into society. She was very good at expressing herself and was a gifted and persuasive writer.

This Victorian style house, built in 1907, remains at 401 S. Church St. The exterior is cedar and pine with mahogany doors. Maple panels with matching trim line the dining room, which also has a European beech wood floor. Following is a picture of the historical marker.
Source: Santa Maria Valley Historical Society collection.

The Smiths had two children: George Clinton Smith Jr. and Margaret Veda Smith. George Smith, who had a go for broke attitude about his business ventures, made and lost a million dollars at least twice in his lifetime. The Smiths had a beautiful home built in 1907 on West Church Street and Thornburgh. It was very much the showplace in town. It had a building in the rear about the size of a garage that was built to house George Junior's toys. Lucretia must have felt like she had married a man much like her father as they weathered the ups and downs of his investments. He made his first million as a bean broker during the Great War. Later Smith did some mining in Mariposa taking his 10-year-old son with him to the mines where they made $1 a day panning for gold. He was nearly 70 years old at the time.

Lucretia died at age 61, preceding her husband who would die in November of 1939. Her health had been failing for several months. Her illness' duration gave her time to think and plan. Her obituary named her "club woman and pioneer resident." She died at the family home at 107 West Park Street. She had for her pallbearers many of the ladies of the valley. Their names were Mesdames Edna Lockwood, Dante Acquistapace, C.W. Rahbar, Hazel Lidbom, Lou Garris and Mabel K. Edwards. Mrs. H.A. Stier conducted the service.

Smith House historic marker
Source: Santa Maria Valley Historical Society collection.

She was survived by her husband, George; her son, George Jr.; and her daughter, Mrs. Margaret V. Davis (later Mrs. William Luke). She also had two grandchildren by her son. Lucretia's daughter, Mrs. William J. Luke, died in December 1940 of pneumonia following the birth of a son who died immediately.

Mrs. Lucretia Smith would be remembered as someone who put women's issues to the forefront where they could be discussed practically in the light of day.

Chapter Five: Splitting Centuries

Virginia Grossini Barca Ziliotto (1884-1949)

Virginia Grossini did not grow up in the valley. She was part of a different kind of new age woman. She was born and grew up in Switzerland. Virginia came to California after her marriage on October 29, 1901. She traveled by ship, then train and arrived speaking no English. She had married Bartolomeo Barca, a man 24 years her senior who was originally from her home village of Aurigeno, Switzerland. Living in America since 1878, Barca had returned to Aurigeno to marry a Swiss girl. He had left behind his childhood sweetheart Victoria Jori, but she had married in his long absence. She also had a 17-year-old daughter, Virginia Grossini.

Virginia Grossini Barca Ziliotto
Source: Janice and Glenn Battles

Virginia and Bartolomeo purchased a portion of Todos Santos Ranch in 1904 on San Antonio Road (near Orcutt, California). Barca had been working on the ranch prior to their marriage. He must have had a pretty good idea what they would be getting and was well satisfied it was where he wanted to make his life with a family.

As the young wife of a farmer, dairyman and rancher, Virginia was busy sunup-to-sundown. She cooked and cared for every workman on the ranch. With 2,900 acres, that was a sizable responsibility. Virginia would have had plenty of practice as she was the second daughter and third child in a dairy family with ten younger brothers and four younger sisters. Virginia's first child, Peter, was born in 1902. She would have six children; Peter, Albino, Adelina, Mary, Walter and Zilda.

The Barca's enjoyed a lot of successes, but there were hard times too. At one point all of the cattle were lost to Texas fever. They were forced to start all over again. The sons worked on the ranch doing a man's work early on. Peter did not attend high school, and Albino only went for the briefest time. The ranch consisted of farming, cattle and dairy operations. Grains, hay and dry beans were grown in the fields. In addition to ranch operations, there was the orchard to tend, fruit to pick, chickens to feed, eggs to gather, canning and the growing and weeding of the vegetable garden.

Virginia and Bartolomeo would help many immigrate to America from their native Switzerland, both family and friends. They hired them to help on their ranch which they called Todos Santos y San Antonio.

Virginia Grossini Barca Ziliotto
Source: Janice and Glenn Battles.

Chapter Five: Splitting Centuries

Virginia Grosini Barca Ziliotto
Source: Santa Maria Valley Historical Society collection.

Bartolomeo built his wife a beautiful home in the Los Alamos Valley in the 1920s. It was a most wonderful home, but it was known that Bartolomeo never wanted to leave the ranch. However, he was persuaded to make a voyage in 1921 to take his wife and their six kids by ship to visit their grandparents and extended family (Virginia had siblings born after she left in 1901) in Aurigeno, Canton Ticino, Switzerland.

Bartolomeo never learned to drive, but Virginia did! She enjoyed it immensely. Images of Virginia racing down the dirt roads with dust flying are firmly imprinted on the memory of her family and neighbors. Bartolomeo would travel by horse between the ranches he owned. He had been able to acquire lands around the state of California and a ranch in Arizona where he grew crops. When grass was scarce on his home ranch, he would ship cattle to Arizona to feed on the grasses there.

Bartolomeo died in 1932 and his sons Peter and Albino took over as the Barca Brothers.

Virginia, now a widow was a doting grandmother. She was short in stature and round. She always brought donuts, gum or candy to her grandchildren, when she visited the ranch, much to the chagrin of her own children.

Her life was characterized by many successes. She was quite the entrepreneur and controlled numerous properties on her own after her husband passed. She enjoyed shopping in Los Angeles and San Francisco, and often she drove herself! She also loved to entertain family and friends. She often would go to the beach with friends and relatives. She was a member of the Minerva Club, Swiss Federation, Catholic Daughters, Altar Society and Companions of Woodcraft.

Virginia found a second husband in Italian widower Elario Ziliotto more recently of Lompoc. She lived in Lompoc from 1940-1947. They were living in Santa Maria when Virginia suffered a major cardiac event and died in 1949. She was 64 years old.

Virginia Grosini Barca Ziliotto, driving
Source: Santa Maria Valley Historical Society collection.

Chapter Five: Splitting Centuries

Ethel Elma Pope (1885-1969)

Ethel Elma Pope
Source: Santa Maria Valley Historical Society collection.

Ethel was born in Oxford, Nebraska, on November 1st, 1885, the oldest of three children. Her parents were from Ohio. Her father was a conductor for a railroad. It was said of her that she had a warm and engaging personality. She was hard to forget.

Ethel graduated high school in McCook, Red Willow, Nebraska, in 1902 as class poet. She headed to college. Higher education was originally intended and designed for men from colonial America times. Elementary education was always widespread. The Puritans, who were instrumental in founding early America, often referred to as New England, believed one should study the Bible to gain a thorough understanding of how to live life. In order to study the Bible, boys and girls were taught to read at an early age. Each New England town was required to pay for a primary school. Secondary schooling was not often attended as children who could work in the fields or around the farmhouse were seen to have a higher calling once the basics of reading and writing were achieved. In some instances, schooling was totally dispensed with as reading and writing could be taught at home if the parents themselves could read and write. By 1750, nearly 90% of New England's women, and almost all of its men, could read and write. This was well above the 60% average in their native England. There was still no higher education for women until later in the 1800s and, even then, it was rare. Coinciding with the beginnings of the first wave of feminism in the 20th century came the attempt by women to gain equal rights to education.

Rare, however, didn't mean none. Ethel E. Pope graduated from the University of Nebraska in 1906. In her college yearbook, the *Sombrero*, she listed her interests as dancing and roller skating. She also announced her intention to teach after graduation.

In 1910, she was living with her family in the Denver, Colorado, area and was teaching in public school. An English major, she especially enjoyed teaching drama and journalism. For the next few years, Ethel moved around practicing and enriching her teaching skills. She was in El Centro, California, for 2 years teaching, then back to Colorado and then on to Nevada. In 1920 Ethel was teaching high school and living with her widowed mother Laura and her sister Jessie, who was also a teacher and employed at the State University in Reno, Nevada.

Ethel Elma Pope
Source: Santa Maria Valley Historical Society collection.

Chapter Five: Splitting Centuries

In August of 1920, Ethel Pope arrived in Santa Maria, California. A new high school building was needed and the community was in debate over the issue. There was also a need and desire for a high school newspaper. Ethel's junior English class voted to take up the responsibility of publishing a school paper every Friday. A name for the paper was also needed. Julia Beeson (Smith) would have the honor of naming the school newspaper, when she casually remarked on a typical windy, spring day, "we should call it the *Breeze*." And so it was. Expenses were covered by a 25-cent per term subscription fee.

Ethel also became advisor for the high school yearbook, the *Review*. She continued to do this through 1929. She then served as advisor for the junior college annual, the *Mascot*, until 1936.

Ethel's first year at the high school was industrious by many standards. By the end of the first year she had also started the Association of Girls Students, later called the Girls League, and was advisor through 1944. Her second year at the high school, Ethel organized the Drama and Arts Club. In January of 1923, the new school building and auditorium, which there had been such a squabble about when she arrived, was finished and ready to be occupied. Ethel became assistant principal and Dean of Girls in 1926.

Many productions would be staged in the auditorium over the next years. Outstanding performances by students and sometimes including Ethel in roles herself. Ethel's students crowded the facility with their performances. So popular were these presentations that, even during the Great Depression, audiences would pack the house willing to pay the $1 to see the performances.

After school hours also included volunteering. She worked for both the draft and ration boards, performed advisory work for clubs and organizations and did extensive letter writing to former students. Over her years working with students, she had earned the reputation of being "absolutely and unconditionally fair." So while she dedicated much of her time to war efforts, she also corresponded with some of the evacuated Japanese.

In 1951, Ethel retired ending a long and distinguished career at Santa Maria Union High School. She moved to Reno, Nevada, to live with her sister Jessie Pope, who had a house that was dubbed "The Vatican." Ethel had lived modestly with Mr. Albert P. Catlin, a car salesman, and his wife, at 529 Cook Street in Santa Maria since 1930.

The high school auditorium was dedicated in 1964 as Ethel Pope Auditorium. The lady herself passed in 1969 at age 83, but her prestigious stage has remained a jewel in Santa Maria although the 1922 building has faced many renewals and refurbishments over its history.

Ethel Pope Auditorium
Source: Santa Maria Valley Historical Society collection.

Mary Lola Paulding (1887-1976)

Mary Lola Paulding
Source: Santa Maria Valley Historical Society collection.

When the Pauldings arrived in Santa Maria in 1892, there were wooden sidewalks and approximately 400 people living in town. 45 years old, Flora Paulding, Mary's mother, was the oldest woman with a college degree. Flora Sackett was born in Ohio in 1847. Unfortunately, her mother died three months after Flora's birth, and her older sister would pass the next year. Robert Sackett, Flora's father, would remarry, and Flora would grow up in Normal, Illinois, where she lived through the American Civil War. Mary's father, Ormond, a medical doctor, had been born to medical, missionary parents in Damascus, Syria, in 1845. Ormond Paulding, at only 19 joined the Union Army with the Ohio 69th Infantry during the war between the states. Surviving the war only re-enforced his call to medicine. He and Flora, who was working as a teacher, married in Delaware, Ohio, on Christmas Eve in 1879. They lived in Illinois for a few years, and Mary's older sister, Ormonde (Ormie), was born there in 1883.

Ormond's brother, Edwin, was in California singing its praises. Ormond and Flora decide to head west and join him. They traveled in a small buggy most of the way camping their way across the vast distance. It was a very difficult course, and the Pauldings eventually sold their buggy and crossed the remaining distance by train. In 1885, the Paulding's arrived in Arroyo Grande, California. Working with his brothers in the medical trade, the Paulding family settled into a Central Coast lifestyle on Cherry Street, where Flora delivered twin girls, Mary Lola and Christina Litti in August of 1887.

> Reconstruction was not an easy time for the North or the South. The Union victory in the Civil War in 1865 may have given over four million slaves freedom, but the process of rebuilding the South during the Reconstruction period (1865-1877) presented a new collection of significant challenges. These challenges made the West look even more of a paradise for those conflicted over the ever-changing social landscape.

Twin sisters Mary and Litti Paulding
Source: Santa Maria Valley Historical Society collection.

By age 5, Mary was already playing nurse, practicing her skills on animals that crossed her path and bandaging up neighborhood children for both real and imagined boo-boos. As a young adult, she took formal nurses training at General Hospital in Los Angeles, where she would spend eight hours a day on the floor training. The training program provided little-to-no pay, and when her daily work was done, she had four hours of classroom study to complete. In 1910 she was finishing her training in a Los Angeles emergency hospital. She received her nurse's cap in February 1911. She returned home to Santa Maria and began working with her father on house calls. She often lived with some of his patients during their recuperation and did light housekeeping and cooked meals. By 1914, she was practicing some on her own, lived at 119 West Cook Street and is one of only four women listed in the Santa Maria phone book as a nurse.

The United States entered the Great War on April 6, 1917, joining its allies: Britain, France, and Russia. Under the command of Major General John J. Pershing, more than two million U.S. soldiers fought on battlefields in France. The American Red Cross recruited 22,000 nurses to serve in the U.S. Army between 1917-1919. Mary decided to sign-up in 1918. She entered and served without rank or commission. She had her Army training from April to August at the Letterman Army Hospital at the San Francisco Presidio. By September she shipped out to France with the American Expeditionary Forces working at a hospital on the Meuse-Argonne front. She returned on-board the S.S. Caronia from France, leaving on February 25 and docking in New York March 6, 1919.

Mary Paulding at Verdun, 1918
Source: Santa Maria Valley Historical Society collection.

After the war she continued to make home nursing her career but took time to work at the nurses' station for the filming of Cecil B. DeMille's *The Ten Commandments* at the Guadalupe Dunes in 1923.

In the 1930s, Mary spent her time at Mrs. Gregory's Santa Maria County Hospital. A polio epidemic appeared each summer in at least one part of the country. Part of the treatment was placing patients into an iron lung. Polio had been around since prehistory but reared its ugliness in spasms of epidemics in the warm summer months wherever it chose. It took children and adults in varying degrees and was poorly understood. Mary would spend hours in the hospital rubbing the patient's arms and legs trying to return feeling to paralyzed limbs. As the disease was such a mystery and known to be contagious, at the end of the day, all hospital employees had to bathe and change clothes before leaving work. She continued to put patient welfare ahead of any fears she might have had for herself.

It was reported that Mary had a gruff side to her nature, but, if true, it never exhibited itself when she was with her patients. She was genuinely compassionate and carried herself with impeccable, professional aplomb. If anyone in the Valley took sick, the word was put out, "Get Mary!"

In 1972, Mary moved to Hanford, California to be near her twin sister Litti and an "adopted sister," Nancy Paulding. Ormie had died of lung cancer in the 1950s. When Mary and Litti could no longer look out for themselves, they entered a nursing home where Mary passed away in 1976 at the age of 88. Her twin, Litti, died a month later.

Mary gave her entire being to caring for others. She provided more than just patient care; she educated patients and family members about current health conditions and provided the medications and treatments needed throughout their lives. She was available to give emotional support and advice to patients and their families through epidemics or the simple common cold. She also took time to work with healthy people providing preventative health care information on maladies that could harm them, both known and newly discovered. Mary had set a high standard of care, and she exceeded everyone's expectations.

Chapter Five: Splitting Centuries

Angelina Linda Pertusi Ontiveros (1894-1998)

Erlinda Ontiveros
From the cover of San Ramon Chapel Pioneers and Their California Heritage, by Erlinda Ontiveros.

Erlinda gave Santa Maria Valley descendants the greatest genealogical gift possible when she published her book *San Ramon Chapel Pioneers and their California Heritage*. Erlinda would live until just three days short of her 104th birthday, and she put them all to good use.

Angelina Linda Ontiveros, second of five children, was born December 12th, 1894, in Foxen Canyon, near the historic Benjamin Foxen adobe. The home was in an isolated area five miles south of San Ramon Chapel. Essentially isolated, the family was almost entirely self-sufficient but had no running water. Her mom had to bucket water in from a well. Erlinda and her siblings were so shy that they often hid when the occasional visitor called. Further isolating them was that the family spoke only Swiss-Italian.

At age 5, Erlinda was sent to school with her older brother, Jim. She and Jim were enrolled in Highland School with Mrs. Richardson as their teacher. Erlinda needed to learn better English, and Jim needed the moral support. The two went barefooted and wearing new shirts and bib-overalls ordered from a Sears and Roebuck catalogue. Lunch was packed in red-striped bucket-like tin boxes with handles, previously containing Dixie Tobacco. Her father, Filippo, took them to school in a horse-and-buggy but left them at the bottom of the hill.

Being so introverted, she and Jim, while willing to walk the rest of the distance across the yard to the school, remained outside the schoolhouse the first week. Neither the teacher nor other children could persuade them to enter. At one point, a teacher tried to force Erlinda into the classroom. She wrestled loose, and by means of some very colorful language that she had heard her father use, let the teacher know how she felt about that style of inducement. The next week, Erlinda's mother accompanied her children into the schoolhouse staying until the classroom children began singing. The joyfulness and happiness displayed by the other children through music relieved all of Erlinda's concerns, and school ceased to be a fearful dread.

School actually became a happy place for Erlinda. In fact, it gifted her with her very name. She had been baptized Linda. When young Linda Pertusi attended Suey School, the teacher Flora McNeil added "Er" to Linda, and, without comment, she accepted the name. Erlinda was bashful, but she knew her own mind; she liked the change and took it by choice for the rest of her life.

Erlinda graduated from Santa Maria Union High School in 1914. She followed high school with Los Angeles Normal, traveling by train from Guadalupe to Los Angeles. She received her diploma in 1916 and then obtained her Elementary Teaching Certificate from Santa Barbara County

Chapter Five: Splitting Centuries

Superintendent of Schools, M.V. Lehner. There was a vacancy at Garey School; Erlinda was accepted for the job. After two years, she applied for a California State Life Diploma.

After her graduation from Normal, she had returned home to the Houk Ranch, where she lived from 1907-1929. As a single woman, she lived at home but drove the horse-and-buggy to Garey for entertainment. She took part in the Portuguese community events attending many parties known as Chamaritas (Portuguese folk music). She also enjoyed numerous barbecues during Pentecost Season. She went to Swiss parties too. Erlinda loved to dance, was pretty good, and never had any difficulty finding a partner.

Erlinda would say she never dated her husband, Porfirio F. Ontiveros. She had known him for seven years before their marriage. They met at community, home and school parties. Such parties and dances were large and everyone was welcome; invitations were often by word of mouth and passed from neighbor-to-neighbor.

Erlinda's father did not approve of "Porfy." He was not of the same nationality as her family. Erlinda would drive to meet him in Sisquoc at her married sister's house. They attended all the public dances and receptions meeting at the dance halls.

During the early 1900s, teachers had to attend Teachers Institute for a week in Santa Barbara. In December of 1929, she drove to the training in a Chevrolet Coupe and stayed at the Carrillo Hotel.

After she finished her mandatory training that year, at age 35, she married Francisco Porfirio Ontiveros at the Santa Barbara Mission. They would spend the next 56 years together, until his death in 1985.

Erlinda taught school professionally for 30 years in the rural towns and schools of the east Santa Maria Valley: Garey, Suey, Olive and Rice. She retired in 1950. Most of her career was spent in one-room school houses, where she was the only teacher and taught every subject to students of all ages. Erlinda was blessed with a remarkable memory. She remembered every family that had lived in the Garey-Sisquoc-Tepusquet area over her lifetime and the names of every student she taught.

Retirement for Erlinda meant the beginning of another endeavor, *San Ramon Chapel Pioneers and Their California Heritage*. Her book contains 56 family genealogies, the history of the communities and schools in the area, plus a history of the San Ramon Chapel and a listing of the cemetery burials. She would spend at least ten hours a day for two years, documenting her book.

Available for research at the Santa Maria Historical Society Museum.

Erlinda had a long and productive life; and she took the opportunity to reminisce with family and friends as her years grew long. From the shy girl, reluctant to enter her first classroom, to becoming an educated classroom teacher, Erlinda relished every day of her long life. Erlinda wrote: "My mother (Domitilla Teresa Milani) used to tell me, 'There was an old lady who hated to die because she learned something every day.' I guess one could say I'm the old lady she was talking about!"

Suey School in 1893 on Dominion Road. Erlinda P. Ontiveros taught in this one-room school house from 1919 to 1923.
Source Santa Maria Valley Historical Society collection.

Chapter Five: Splitting Centuries

Odulia Anna Carranza Dille (1897-1990)

Odulia Carranza is the great-granddaughter of Juan Pacifico and Martina Ontiveros; Martina being Eduarda Foxen's twin sister. Odulia was practically Santa Maria royalty with such a great valley lineage. She was one of eight children born to Rose Ontiveros and Feliz Carranza, who were married in 1885. She was born in Mendoza Canyon and raised in Miguel Canyon; locations in the Sisquoc area. Her mother passed away in 1901 at age 44 leaving eight children, ages 1-to-14. Odulia was four at her mother's death.

Odulia attended Olive School in Sisquoc completing the 8th grade. She was living on Garey Road in 1910 with her widowed father, who supported on the farm by her uncle, Napoleon Ontiveros. Her older brothers were also employed on the farm while her sisters Inez, at twenty, and Margaret, at nineteen, were taking care of all of the other children.

In 1916, Odulia Carranza walked into the Lucas Sanitarium and asked nurse Jane Lang, who was operating the hospital at that time, if she could apply for training. She had sought out Mrs. Lang on the advice of Dr. Bert Coblentz, who sent her to Lang upon hearing Odulia describe her desire to be a doctor. Unfortunately for Odulia, an 8th grade education wasn't a stepping stone toward college and a medical license, but it was the beginning of a wonderful and fulfilling career in nursing.

Mrs. Lang was a talented nurse and instructor. Despite not receiving the book knowledge that school educated nurses received, Odulia had the benefit of hands-on learning from a highly skilled nurse. Odulia could soon work alongside any school instructed nurse and shine professionally. In short order, Odulia was functioning as a fully qualified nurse, caring for patients, dispensing medicines and assisting in the operating room, where she eventually became a surgical nurse and performed duties around the operating table assisting the surgeon with both elective and life-saving procedures. She was also sometimes the anesthesiologist.

Dr. Lucas Sanitarium, 722 S. Broadway, c. 1917, later converted to other uses. This was eventually the location of Perko's Restaurant, and, at the time of this writing, The Pantry Restaurant.
Source: Santa Maria Valley Historical Society collection.

The 12-beds hospital at 722 South Broadway staffed four nurses working in pairs. A standard shift was twelve hours that more often than not stretched into sixteen. Odulia could do everything that was required and sometimes that included lesser tasks like janitorial work and diaper washing. Nurses were given quarters in a separate building behind the hospital. They had their meals family-style in the hospital kitchen. To Odulia's delight, and probably with her encouragement, her older sister Inez began sharing a room with her and taking nurses training courses.

Odulia was well accomplished by 1918 when the influenza epidemic struck. She worked with the local Santa Maria physicians to convert the old Princess Hall on Pine Street into an infirmary so that those highly contagious cases were kept well away from patients who were confined to hospital beds for other maladies.

On April 10, 1918, Odulia would be working at the sanitarium helping deliver a son to Frances and Fremont Dille. The baby was named Lloyd, and Odulia had no idea that the small boy would one day call her mom.

In 1921 Monte Dille, as he was known, returned to the Lucas Sanitarium to visit his sister who was a patient. Monte was separated from his wife, Lloyd's mother, and working in the Taft oil fields. The courtship began, centered around rides in his Model-T Ford, with trips to silent movies at Santa Maria's Gaiety Theatre. Saturday nights they drove to Sisquoc to dance. On January 14, 1923, Monte and Odulia were married.

Odulia, Monte and Lloyd moved to Long Beach. The oil business was booming, and Monte went where work took him. Odulia had never left the Valley before and was quite homesick. She shared in an interview (from 1979) that she cried every day she was away from Santa Maria. It wasn't long before Monte brought his family back home.

Odulia Dille with Lloyd.
Source: Santa Maria Valley Historical Society collection.

On October 19, 1924, Odulia was admitted to the Lucas Sanitarium. She became the second woman in the Valley to have a caesarian delivery. She gave birth to son, Harold Lee Dille, that day. Unfortunately for the Dille's, "our darling baby," as his headstone would read, died on December 4th of the same year.

As the time went by, Odulia's schedule stayed demanding. Although she was never able to get a *bona fide* nursing school education, she kept very busy. Eventually the Lucas Sanitarium closed, but Jane Lang and Jessie Grigsby started a new hospital. Odulia worked there as a special duty nurse, alongside Mary Paulding and Ione Haslam.

Odulia had the soul of a healer. She loved nursing. Caring for people was in her nature, and nursing was its best expression. She would wear the starched whites of a nurse for more than 50 years. The joy of watching patients recover fulfilled her, and she loved working with the doctors and other nurses.

Chapter Five: Splitting Centuries

In 1949 Lloyd Dille died suddenly, but Odulia was by his side. She had been there for his first breath, and she was present for his last. Odulia continued her work as a nurse finding her own healing in helping others. Lloyd had two daughters and a son, who were also of great solace in those first days after his loss. Odulia and Monte would eventually have seven great grandsons and two great granddaughters.

Monte and Odulia were avid outdoorsmen most of their marriage. They loved camping and fishing in the High Sierras, but as the years went by, they remained closer to home and their grandchildren. Odulia, although considered retired, really never was. Someone always needed care, and where there was a need, there you would always find Odulia.

Monte passed in 1982 and Odulia in 1990. In reflection the only regret that she reported was that she didn't try harder to become a surgeon. They are buried together in the Santa Maria Cemetery with little Harold Lee close beside them.

Odulia A. Dille gravestone, Santa Maria Cemetery
Source: www.findagrave.com

Chapter Six: Coming of Age in a New Century

Women were slowly changing their roles in the world, and, in so doing, revolutionizing the entire world! War, poverty, politics and just general umbrage with the *status quo* had given women the incentive to seek new powers! In America, a new image of womanhood was emerging as the 19th century closed, and the 20th century dawned. Women didn't look the same, and it was this new image that began shaping public views of a woman's role in society. New "tags" identified the ladies of this time: Gibson Girl, suffragist, a Bohemian feminist, college girl, flapper. Collectively these images came to epitomize the modern woman. This modern woman represented a female generation that came from the time between 1890 and 1920. She would challenge gender norms and roles by asserting her presence through work, education, entertainment, and politics. She spoke differently, and she denoted a distinctly modern look that contrasted with the old Victorian ideals of her mother.

The modern woman not only perpetuated the rise of feminism and campaigned for women's suffrage, she was recognized in a new realm, consumerism. The market place and the robust economy didn't miss the modern woman as an avid shopper with control of discretionary cash. Cars had been produced solely in the color black until woman entered the market! Henry Ford did not want to paint cars any color except black. His wife and son forced him into meeting the demands of women in the marketplace. Women were advancing their own causes and engaged in the economy as their dollars were ringing up in cash registers for not just basics but extras!

On Broadway looking north toward Main Street, c. 1920

Source: Santa Maria Valley Historical Society collection.

Chapter Six: Coming of Age in a New Century

Ethel May Palmer Dorsey Conrad (1902-1991)

Ethel May Palmer Dorsey Conrad
Source: Santa Maria Valley Historical Society collection.

Ethel Palmer was born into a minister's home in a sleepy little town, Long Prairie, Minnesota. She was named for her mother's sister, Ethel May Clark. Always just Ethel until she reached high school when she learned this, she decided then to be known as Ethel May.

Her father was the Reverend William George Palmer, and her mother was the former Ora Matilda Clark. The family moved to California in 1903 and although she would travel, Ethel May always called California home.

Ethel May was a bright, inquisitive, and creative child. She enjoyed being part of a big extended family, lots of aunts and uncles. There were times when missionaries from Japan visited her home. With a father who was a highly respected minister, she enjoyed a lot of praise and attention. Ethel May had a big world for a little girl growing up in the early years of a new century, but that was about to change. In an age when public appearances mattered, her parents divorced. It was represented to Ethel May in terms like, "it would have been better if there had been a death in the family, than a divorce." Somewhere around 1920, the life that she and her siblings understood and enjoyed changed dramatically. Her mother, Ora, charged her father, Will Palmer, with philandering. Ethel May actually witnessed the moment of confrontation from her piano stool. She felt incredible sadness as she lay awake all night after the incident listening to her mother sob through the night. The following morning, Ora Palmer packed up her prized possessions and moved them next door to be stored in a neighbor's basement. She and the children walked away from that home forever. Ethel May felt the stigma of divorce severely. Her mother was unrelenting in refusing to let the children see their father and didn't allow him to be mentioned in the house. Ethel May adored her father, and she and her brothers found that, through relatives, they could still see him on occasion. Nothing was ever the same: her extended family had all kinds of opinions, and Ethel May wondered why all the adults in her life didn't understand forgiveness the same way she did.

Ethel May enrolled in Manual Arts High School in Los Angeles. She wanted to be an artist. She had her first art lessons from her Aunt Ida who taught her to paint in water colors and oil, she also painted china. She was talented. She was even asked by the head of the Art Department to represent the school on a Saturday morning at Hamburger's Department Store (later known as May Company). She was to do silhouettes of small children for which she was paid $1 an hour, very good recompense at the time.

Ethel May, although an art major, soon became interested in an even more creative art form, theatre arts. In truth she had always been interested in theatre. Any opportunity she would volunteer to perform as a singer, an actress, or a public speaker. In the early 1920s, she began dabbling in singing

Chapter Six: Coming of Age in a New Century

on the radio. Her uncle Elmer introduced her to the KFOX station manager in Long Beach. She made trips there on the Red Car Line on weekends to sing one group of songs staying overnight at her grandfather's house. For Ethel May, it was when the station manager introduced her as "Miss Palmer, our contralto" that she felt she might have a career. Ethel May decided she would not marry until she had a singing vocation.

This decision propelled Ethel May through college. She worked in a secretarial position to help finance her college education and the very costly vocal lessons that she was taking. It was this job that first introduced her to Christian Science. She would maintain her allegiance to this practice all of her life.

She changed her course of study many times: art, then music, then a kindergarten course. All were teacher training courses, which was one of only a few preferred professions for a proper lady: teacher, nurse, and secretary.

Ethel May's intention had been to attend USC, but her mother insisted that she attend a Presbyterian College, Occidental. She made the most of the opportunity by living away from home and selecting off campus housing versus a dormitory so that she could have access to a piano every day. She was already studying both voice and piano by the time she started her junior year. As it turned out, "Mother knew best!" Occidental was wonderful, and she gained great experience as a soloist with the Women's Glee Club. She also joined the women's debate team. When her life as a student ended in 1926, her Bachelor of Arts certificate only inspired her more toward seeking knowledge and renewed her concentration on her vocal studies. She was determined, above all else, to be a professional singer and gain vocal recognition.

Her first professional opportunity was with the Florentine Trio, a group which was on the California vaudeville circuit. While this group was far from her first choice, she realized she must gain stage experience in the professional theatre. As the name indicated, there was an Italian element. They wore Italian costumes and sang songs in Italian. Their engagements took them up and down the California

Ethel May Palmer graduates from Occidental College
Source: Reaching for High C by Ethel-May Conrad.

coast. One of her early engagements was in Santa Maria, where she appeared at the Gaiety Theater on East Main Street. After her performance the owner introduced himself and invited the group out for a Chinese supper. This middle aged, sandy haired gentleman was Mr. Harry Dorsey.

Harry Dorsey wasted no time in securing a life with Ethel May Palmer although 24 years her senior. Ethel May had found all the young men in her life without direction and never taking her desire to be a professional performer seriously. Not Harry; he was what she wanted. Ethel May couldn't believe her luck, a happy marriage and a career. Dorsey proposed on the golf course at Pebble Beach. It wasn't the first time he had talked about marrying, "my brown-eyed singin' girl," but it was the time she accepted.

Ethel May Palmer Dorsey Conrad
Source: Santa Maria Valley Historical Society collection.

Ethel May's life was filled with extras and extravagances. A honeymoon in Honolulu was followed by a new home, which was completely furnished when she arrived, at 1010 South Broadway. Included was a baby grand piano in the living room. The year is 1927, and Ethel May settled into a life in Santa Maria. She was not idle and became a part of almost every important activity in the town.

In 1928 she also became a mother. Harry C. Dorsey, Jr., was born in October of that year. Shortly after his birth, Ethel May got right back to her daily vocal practicing. There were continual requests for her to sing for churches, clubs, weddings and funerals. Her husband decided she needed more focus, and Ethel May started training with Mebane Beasley, a vocal coach in Santa Barbara. He changed her vocal life, helping her to lift her voice up the scale to F above high C.

To some degree, encouraging Ethel May to train more was a ruse. Harry loved everything about Ethel May, but he not was so much behind her singing career as she initially thought. He had ways of distracting her from her career, but they were wonderful ways! He took her traveling. Ethel May loved an adventure almost as much as the stage. In 1931 when Harry was elected Santa Maria Rotary Club president, he was sent to Vienna as a delegate to the International Rotary Convention. Ethel May accompanied him. They sailed aboard a British liner. Harry surprised her by giving her name to the entertainment committee that then invited her to sing for several occasions. Harry was a smart guy.

In 1932, Ethel May was delighted to find many musicians and music lovers in the Santa Maria. One of her finds was the wealthy industrialist and philanthropist, George Allan Hancock. He wanted to contribute to the community's cultural enrichment. He decided to produce the opera *Carmen*. He employed William Strobridge to direct the production and conduct the Community Orchestra. Besides two professional singers from Los Angeles who sang the roles of Don Jose and Escamillo, the other singers and dancers were local talent. Julia Smith became the fiery Carmen and Ethel sang the role of Micaela, Don Jose's sweetheart. The opera was staged in the high school auditorium (later the Ethel Pope Auditorium) to a packed house.

Chapter Six: Coming of Age in a New Century

Ethel May continued her singing career, performing in Santa Maria, Santa Barbara, San Francisco and southern California cities. She also continued to sing at churches, clubs, weddings and funerals! In June 1933, Ann Elizabeth Dorsey arrived to complete the family.

Ethel May Dorsey did a lot to help Santa Maria grow culturally. Civic minded she participated in clubs like the Minerva Club, serving as president in 1938, but she started important programs as well. She was willing to share ideas, and she was also willing to be the chair of committees, to fundraise for her ideas, and to recruit others to join her in worthwhile endeavors.

In 1942 in support of the United States Troops in World War II, Ethel May organized and directed the Volunteer Special Services of the American Red Cross. She traded her life as a performing artist to become a business executive. She conducted several Red Cross fund drives. Her first USO fund drive featured Mrs. Spencer Tracy, who came from Los Angeles to be the featured guest speaker at the banquet. Ethel May served with the Red Cross throughout the war. She also planted a victory garden as food shortages and rationing became prevalent. She organized and directed Nurses' Aides, Gray Ladies, Canteen Corps, Motor Corps and Staff Assistants. She had a lot of help; other wives in the community joined her chairing the new programs and perpetuating the mission and ideals of each group.

Santa Maria, as a community, was strong. Around 10,000 folks were pulling together through all kinds of challenges. A generation was passing, and Ethel May had enjoyed the stories of the original pioneers. She now wanted to write a book as much as she had ever wanted to sing.

Source: "Reaching for High C" by Ethel May Conrad

She began by interviewing members of Santa Maria's pioneer families. While in personal conversation with them, she came to realize they wanted an historical society. Ethel May found a way to make this happen. In 1955, the City of Santa Maria was to celebrate its Golden Anniversary. Mayor Leonard Petersen asked Ethel May to be chairman of the Golden Anniversary Committee. She agreed and in the back of her mind knew this was the pathway to creating an historical society for Santa Maria. Once again Ethel May was a big success; the society was formed, and, in 1959, the book *This Is Our Valley* came off the presses. With a little help and a lot of effort, Ethel May had her book.

Harry Dorsey died in 1961. Ethel May remarried in 1969 to Walter E. Conrad. She was one of a kind: a most remarkable person, an active leader in Santa Maria all of her days, civic and social. She was cofounder of the Community Orchestra; cofounder and president of the Santa Maria Valley Historical Society, charter president of Santa Maria Valley Beautiful, and Woman of the Year for 1967. She died at 89 in her home. She left very little undone. Her list of achievements could fill a book, and they have. It's called *Reaching for High C*, available to view at the Santa Maria Valley Historical Society research library.

Chapter Six: Coming of Age in a New Century

Olga Pauline Giacomini Weldon (1903-2006)

Olga Weldon's parents: Paul Giacomini and Edith Grisingher, 1902.
Source: Santa Maria Valley Historical Society collection.

Olga was born 20 April, 1903, in Guadalupe, California. Her father, Paul Giacomini, was Swiss-Italian, born in 1876. He immigrated in 1896. He married Edith Matilda Grisingher of San Luis Obispo in 1902. Olga was the oldest child. She had a sister and a brother: Irene and Ernest. Unfortunately for Olga, her mother died at age 27, only a week after her brother's birth in 1908. Olga was five years old. Paul Giacomini was a butcher with his own shop on Guadalupe Street in 1910. He later worked the stockyards as both a dealer and cattle raiser. He had one of the first cars in the Santa Maria Valley. He often took Olga and her sisters on drives to Foxen Canyon where he had cattle. Roads were more suggestions, and, on one occasion, Olga's sister Irene bounced out of the car! He remarried in 1909 and had another daughter, Lela, but was widowed again in 1919 before he passed at the age of 44 in 1920.

Olga seldom ventured far from her valley roots. While many pioneer families travelled hard and far to be residents, Olga was born here. She attended elementary school in Guadalupe, and, after college, she attended Immaculate Heart College in Los Angeles. She worked as a cashier at the Security First National Bank in Guadalupe. She lived through a bank robbery and later witnessed one of the biggest disasters in Guadalupe history when much of the town burned down in the 1920s.

Olga experienced Santa Maria when Stowell Road was the end of town and a cemetery and endless agriculture filled the rest of the landscape. She married Thomas Patrick Weldon in 1927. They had two sons together: Richard Paul and Thomas Patrick, Jr. Weldon Sr. was six-foot tall, brown haired with a light complexion and hazel eyes. The young Utah born attorney purchased them a home on W. Pershing Street, and, for the next 70 years, Olga bore witness to the evolution of the valley.

Born when the population was close to 1,000, Olga was a witness to every major change for nearly a century. It would require great imagination for any of the current 110,000 plus residents to imagine our valley without paved roads, multiple schools, highways, churches, or movie theaters. Olga watched as gas lamps became electric lamps, outhouses disappeared from the everyday landscape, horses changed to automobiles, pencils became computers, letters were replaced with email, never locking a door turned into home security systems, and cooking from scratch transitioned to canned and frozen food.

Passport Picture, October 1929
Source: Santa Maria Valley Historical Society collection.

Olga Pauline Giacomini Weldon
Source: Santa Maria Valley Historical Society collection.

She and her sisters were very supportive of agriculture. They owned a ranch that was used for many years as a dairy and later for growing vegetables and then strawberries. Some of her favorite tenants were Dennis Spazzadeschi and Emilio Sutti, who operated dairies; the Freitas brothers, who grew the vegetables; and Tak, Kingo and Tets Furukawa, who cultivated the strawberries.

Olga Weldon was an active member of the Minerva Club and dedicated volunteer for the Marian Medical Auxiliary. In her senior years she became an avid horticulturist, well known for her beautiful roses, camellias and begonias.

Olga was a Santa Maria Valley girl. She remembered a time when a single orange was a good Christmas gift and any ride in a car was "damned uncomfortable." She lived through the "war to end all wars," knew the hardships of the Great Depression, listened on radio to the unfolding of events in December 1941, used black out curtains hoping to confuse the enemy and avoid a coastal invasion during WWII, and watched black-and-white television coverage of the moon landing and John F. Kennedy's assassination and then every other major televised event in color through the 9-11 attack. She lived through 20 different Santa Maria mayors. She watched the town torn down and a mall built. She lamented the closing of the Santa Maria Club, where she enjoyed polenta dinners and card games with friends.

She could tell a good yarn; family said most stories began, "Oh, brother." She had a way of sharing a unique perspective with colorful commentary. Living a century in one place made her viewpoint significant and essential to understanding the development of our town. Every building, from the high school to the court house, held important memories for Olga. She believed a life close to family and in proximity to childhood friends, who in some ways became extended family, was a life well spent.

If asked if she wished she'd traveled more, her reply was always the same. "Why? The people are friendly here, and it's so pretty. The weather is beautiful. I have everything."

Chapter Six: Coming of Age in a New Century

Thelma Louise Chamberlain Battles (1906-2008)

Thelma Louise Chamberlain Battles college graduation picture.
Source: Glenn Battles

Thelma was born in Santa Barbara January 24, 1906, to Glenn Sumner Chamberlain and Bertha Edith Doty. She was the second of five children. Thelma was also part of a new trend: second generation Californians. Her father was a native of Nebraska, but her mother and her siblings were all California born and, on her mother's side, so was her grandmother.

Her family were fruit farmers, mostly lemons, but, also avocados and walnuts. She graduated from Cathedral Oaks School in Santa Barbara in 1925. She entered Santa Barbara State Teachers College the following year and graduated with a teaching degree in 1928.

In 1930, Thelma was hired to teach in Santa Maria at Pleasant Valley School, the oldest school in Santa Maria. It was a one-room schoolhouse for students in grades 1-8 built by Rudolph Cook in February 1870. She had anywhere from 15-40 students at each enrollment.

Pleasant Valley School was located about one mile from the Battles' homestead where she received room and board as part of her teaching salary. Thelma had the distinction of being the last teacher to teach in the 66-year-old building. The schoolhouse held its last term ending in June of 1936.

Thelma was teaching in an historic setting although probably not that comfortable. The old one room schoolhouse had seen better days.

During her teaching assignment and while living at the Battles farm, she met James (Jim) George Battles. He was the son of Ulysses Grant Battles and Ella Francis Hourihan. Jim Battles was 6'1" with brown hair, hazel eyes and a ruddy complexion. In the autumn of 1868, his grandfather, George Washington Battles, was among the first to arrive in the Santa Maria Valley. Santa Maria was barely 30 years past incorporation, and the Battles were three generations dedicated to the Valley. At age 24 in 1930, Battles was working unpaid on the family ranch as a laborer.

> She also had an additional historical distinction to share with her students: that of being a Mayflower descendant. Her mother bore the name of a famous Mayflower passenger, Edward Doty. Doty arrived in Plymouth with William Bradford in 1620. He was a signatory of the Mayflower Compact. Doty was the indentured servant of Stephen Hopkins. Doty would marry Faith Clark who came to Plymouth in 1630. They would have nine children; all would survive to marry and have children of their own.

Thelma married Jim Battles on January 26, 1937. They had four children, James Jr., Glenn, Myron and Barbara. Thelma continued to work during the child rearing years but only as a substitute teacher. She reserved the majority of her time for her family from the birth of James Jr., on June 3, 1937, through Barbara Jane's arrival March 11, 1941. She would focus on teaching her own children for the next decade.

Chapter Six: Coming of Age in a New Century

In 1951 Thelma Battles returned to teaching full-time. She taught for Blochman School District in Sisquoc. She had combination classes for 3rd-4th and 5th-6th. She would stay behind a desk for the next 20 years at Blochman, retiring in 1972. Thelma was a highly respected educator. Her reputation was as a "tough teacher who found a way to successfully educate all children."

Although Thelma retired from the school system, she had a love for teaching children. As her grandchildren arrived, she played school with them in her home, complete with desks, books and worksheets. She had a passion for learning that she shared with encouragement and love with everyone and was not above taking an opportunity to correct any improper use of grammar when it caught her ear. Thelma could have invented the Trivial Pursuit character Hector, as she enjoyed challenging her family on their knowledge of current and past-history events whenever an opportunity presented.

Thelma Louise Chamberlain Battles
Source: Glenn Battles.

Thelma was married to Jim Battles for 54 years. They spent their entire marriage living on the Battles' family farm at Rosemary and Betteravia roads where they first operated a dairy and then raised hogs. Jim Battles passed in 1990.

Thelma would continue in the valley to the age of 102. She has many descendants still living in the Santa Maria Valley.

Chapter Six: Coming of Age in a New Century

Laura Jane Stair Smith Harris (1914-1982)

Laura Jane Stair on the oil lease.
Source: Santa Maria Valley Historical Society collection.

Jane was born June 4, 1914, in the little town of Bicknell, an oil town created by the Western Union Oil Company, 18 miles south of Santa Maria in the Orcutt Hills area just west of Mount Solomon. Her father, Jay Urban Stair, was superintendent there. Stair had come from Wisconsin after his father's death to find work to support his mother. He arrived at age 19 to find the oil industry on the edge of a boom. Starting as an office boy, he worked his way up to superintendent. He met a beautiful local girl, Lucile Pearl Bryant. Their courtship was centered around their love of the automobile. "No other young couple ever had more fun than we did in those early days of the automobile," Lucile Bryant Stair told her daughter Jane. The young couple gallivanted about the Valley, first in the horse-less carriage, then the steam models, and on up to the latest things in gasoline engines, but it was the sporty Mitchell that was their favorite. After what was considered a long engagement, Lucile and Jay married on May 1, 1912. When the wedding bells died out and the honeymoon ended, the young couple settled into the home in Bicknell for the next seven years. All of their children would be born at home or in the Lucas Hospital in Santa Maria.

Life at Bicknell was noisy. Oil gushers were popping up, and, as a result of this activity, rough oil field camps were developing comprised of several dozen families. The whole area was booming with hurriedly thrown together towns made up of a grocery store, post office, a combination one-room schoolhouse and church.

Jane remembered her father's small office always being stuffed with people, all relating problems to do with the oil business from sump holes and storage tanks to equipment and warehouse issues. There was a piercing whistle atop the boiler house that sounded out at noon each day and again at 5:00 pm. It was this steam whistle that could also create instant terror when it blew off schedule as this meant there was fire and the men were needed to form a fire line. Oil well fires were numerous and frightening. Many times, Jane remembered, she and her mother running from their home toward her father's office to be sure he was safe.

Map showing the town of Bicknel on the oil lease.
Source: Santa Maria Valley Genealogy Society.

Bicknell had no sidewalks, or streets, just roads with oil spills and ruts cut into the ground for one lane of travel. These "pathways" wound through the fields to each of the oil wells and were in constant use. The cattle grazing in the area often came right up onto Jane's front yard. Her father eventually put a fence around their house, but Jane believed it was as much about keeping his "redheads" in as keeping the cows out!

"On the lease," Jane said, "we were referred to as the bosses' kids." All of the Stair kids had flashy red hair, freckles across the nose and a most curious nature. What one didn't think of, the other did. There were many unsupervised moments on the lease that led to amazing stories: dunking the cat in the white paint, chasing a skunk from under the house with a broom handle, or swatting yellow jackets that had swarmed by the hundreds attracted to the fruit for the jams and jellies being prepared in the kitchen.

Laura Jane Stair, South Pasadena High School yearbook picture.
Source: Santa Maria Valley Historical Society collection.

Jane remembered that in those early days, almost any place on the lease, you could hear the chug-chug of the oil wells pumping, and the smell of sulphur. This life was a harsh departure from the city life her mother, Lucile Bryant, had enjoyed; even if she did live in the nicest house, furnished with new furniture and her own piano from her parents' house. Lucile was such an accomplished musician, she could have performed professionally, but while she continued to enjoy enriching those around her with music, she turned her passions to caring for her family.

Life on the oil lease was never dull for a child growing up there! Before Jane had very many recollections of the everyday happenings, a baby brother showed up in December 1915. One of the early memories on the lease was about Christmas trees. "You didn't buy them on a lot ready-made," Jane related. "We searched out our tree on the country hillsides." A selection was made and dragged home usually the day before Christmas.

STAIR, JANE
Atelier—1401 St. Albans.
Perspective—Teaching.
Masterpiece — "A Modern Coquette," Alvarez.
Background—French Club (2) (3) Vice-pres.-Treas. (4); Pendragon (4); Hockey (2) (3); Riding (2).

Laura Jane Stair, South Pasadena High School yearbook.
Source: Santa Maria Valley Historical Society collection.

When the Armistice was signed in 1919 to end The Great War, there was a celebration on the oil lease at Bicknell. Jay Stair played his French horn, and Lucile played the piano, which was pushed onto the front porch. Everyone on the lease came to the house that November night. Jane admitted she had never heard so much noise nor witnessed so much confusion as she tried to understand why everyone had decided to dance and sing and kiss each other. Everyone laughed and was happy. The partying went on long after Jane went to bed, but she clearly remembered the cleaning up the next day.

Jane's days in the Valley were drawing to a close. Three months after her sister, Marian Lucile Stair, was born, the oil business took her family to South Pasadena. Jane graduated high school at South Pasadena High School where in her yearbook she listed her activities as French, hockey and riding. It also suggested she was a "modern coquette." After high school, at 19, she took a trip to England with her father before she attended Pomona College where she met and married Stanley Moore

Chapter Six: Coming of Age in a New Century

Smith on November 6, 1935. Smith was six-foot-tall with blonde hair and blue eyes. There would be two children born: Darwin in 1937 and Sally Ann in 1939. He, like her father, worked in the oil industry for Shell Oil Company, Inc. He was an oil gauger; someone who was responsible for levels in oil tanks, equipment maintenance and production levels. He died during World War II leaving Jane a widow. She would meet again with high school sweetheart Albert E. "Bud" Harris, and this time they would be married.

Jane would be gone from the valley until 1970 when she would return to her roots. Jane's husband had worked in the oil industry "drilling mud." In Santa Maria he would open Shell Service Stations: one at Boone and Broadway and another at 740 Donovan. Jane had great cause to love the Santa Maria Valley. She was the descendent daughter of several Santa Maria pioneers and the great-granddaughter of Harriet Sharp (see Harriet Sharp Hart, above). She was returning to family.

After her return, Jane made her life study understanding her family's history, its presence and its contributions in the valley. She became a member of the South County Historical Society, the Santa Maria Valley Pioneer Association, the Santa Maria Genealogical Society and the Santa Maria Valley Historical Museum.

Hart family home, City Landmark No. 4.
Source: Santa Maria Valley Historical Society collection.

Jane would serve as senior vice president of the historical society in 1978 and as museum curator until illness forced her to step down. She was instrumental in relocating the Hart family home and getting its designation as City Landmark No. 4. It was her efforts through special articles and letters to the editor at the Santa Maria Times that promoted preservation projects of historical buildings.

Lucile Stair, Jane's mother lived to be 95, but Jane was taken by cancer a short nine months later, on November 9, 1982, at the age of 68. Jane had three sons, a daughter and seven grandchildren. Before her death Jane completed a four-volume composition of her family history beginning with Samuel and Hannah Sharp and ending with her mother Lucile's death February 2, 1982. She also wrote many historical vignettes for the Santa Maria Times during her tenure at the Santa Maria Valley Historical Society.

Chapter Six: Coming of Age in a New Century

Patricia Jean Boyd (1920-2012)

Patty was born into a valley heritage; her mother was Gertrude Anne Rice. Maternal grandparents were William Hickman and Florence Lee Coiner Rice. William had arrived at age 17 to the Santa Maria Valley. His parents were John H. and Mary Long Rice (Mary is mentioned earlier as a Valley lady), one of nine families to arrive in 1873. They purchased part of the old Punta de la Laguna rancho near Guadalupe. William immediately went to work with his father to build a fortune from the virgin land. Florence Lee Coiner Rice had a twin sister, Crimora Beauregard Coiner; both gals were named for Confederate generals. Their father was another pioneer to the Valley having been from Virginia and settling in Los Alamos after the American Civil War.

Patricia Jean Boyd
Source: Santa Maria Valley Historical Society collection.

Gertrude Rice married Elmer George Boyd, a local boy who had his roots in the valley as well. His father was Thomas Boyd of Ireland, who arrived in the valley fall of 1874. Elmer Boyd having completed only two years of high school had already taken up farming and so continued after their marriage. Gertrude was a Santa Maria Union High School graduate in 1908 and a University of California, Berkeley, graduate in 1912. She married Boyd sometime between 1912 and 1920. At the time of the 1920 census, they were living as man and wife on a farm in the Santa Maria Valley. In September of that year, a little girl was born to them. Patricia Jean Boyd was small. She would be small in stature all of her days but never in spirit. She had a condition known as achondroplasia, a genetic disorder that results in dwarfism. Her parents christened her in February 1922 as Patricia Grace.

Although divorce followed, Gertrude and Patty took the change in stride. Gertrude moved back to her parents' house with her daughter, and Elmer Boyd moved on to the oil fields and his mother's house.

The Rices never looked upon Patty with anything but love and great expectations. She attended local schools and graduated from Santa Maria Union High School in 1938. When Patty expressed to her grandfather a desire to drive, he encouraged her to figure it out, and she did! She was always encouraged to strive. When her mother remarried, Patty chose to remain at home, until time for college, with the aging grandparents she adored.

Patty attended Wheaton College in Illinois and graduated from San Jose State College with a Bachelor of Arts Degree in music. She did post-graduate work in music at the University of Denver and was a member of Mu Phi Epsilon, a music honor society.

Patty was an amazing pianist. She could dance her fingers up and down the keyboard with ease and elegance. She performed classical music, sacred music, secular music, and popular music effortlessly. In 1945, Patty began teaching piano in Santa Maria at her own studio at 423a Broadway. She took her work seriously and expected her students to do the same. They were not allowed poor posture nor to not practice without getting a stern report and extra instructions. Patty also provided recital opportunities for her students, sometimes in her own home on Mariposa Way. She thus afforded

Chapter Six: Coming of Age in a New Century

them a tangible goal to train towards, the chance to perform before an audience. She believed that recitals provided an opportunity for her students to feel successful and gain great confidence. Perhaps she experienced these benefits herself as she faced the many challenges obstructing her in those early years. Learning piano for anyone requires many, many hours of practice over many, many years. Performances gave both her and her students the recognition they well deserved for their dedication to learning and the honing of their chosen art form. Patty continued as a music teacher for decades and later joined the faculty of Allan Hancock College. At Hancock College, she began teaching advanced piano to selected students. Patty continued as an educator into her late eighties and sustained her involvement with the college until her death at age 91 in July 2012.

Patricia Jean Boyd
Source: Santa Maria Valley Historical Society collection.

Patty Boyd also left an incredible legacy to the Santa Maria Valley at her death. She provided an estimated $10 to $12 million bequest from her estate to the Hancock College music program. It was the largest gift in the history of the Allan Hancock College Foundation and believed to be the second largest donation ever to a California community college. She additionally designated another $1 million for the Pacific Conservatory of the Performing Arts, PCPA.

Patty had proven herself a lifelong patron of the arts and had made it her life's work to bring the arts to the Santa Maria Valley community. Her devotion to music and her dedication to the arts was a gift she gave to herself and then shared generously with others both through instruction and her generous gift. Patty J. Boyd will be remembered as a person of character, a creative spirit, and someone who was a tremendous supporter of the arts, a wonderful educator and an artist at the keyboard.

Chapter Seven: Charitable Societies

Probably the first club for the ladies of the valley was the Ladies Literary Society. We say probably because the ladies gathered in small groups all across the valley doing a variety of tasks for church or home or neighbors from the first moment that there were more than two of them. The ladies of our valley always had in mind to better the community through creating opportunities to enrich themselves and their children.

Minerva Club

There is no club in Santa Maria that has enjoyed a longer life than the Minerva Club. The ladies-only club was first organized under the name Ladies Literary Society on October 5, 1894, by a group of twenty-five women devoted to the idea of making the town a better place in which to live: intellectually, spiritually, and morally. Spirited and with high ideals, the ladies met on a Friday afternoon at the home of Mrs. Mary Smith with Mrs. L. E. Blochman as chairman *pro tem*. Mrs. O. W. Maulsby was secretary. Present that day in addition were Mrs. James F. Goodwin, Minerva Thornburgh, Mrs. T.A. Jones, Mrs. Emma McKenzie, Mrs. Minnie

Minerva Club picnic, c. 1880
Source: Santa Maria Valley Historical Society collection.

Steans, Mrs. W.T. Lucas, Mrs. Ruben Hart, Mrs. Charles Curryer, Mrs. Cora Dickes, Mrs. Madison Thornburgh, Mrs. H.H. Harris, Mrs. John McMillen, Mrs. Caleb Sherman, Mrs. John Weeks, Mrs. C.H. Weaver, Mrs. W. A. Haslam, Mrs. Emma Chaffin, Mrs. Alex Stanley, Mrs. A.E. Lutnesky, Mrs. L. M. Schwabacher, Mrs. E.T. Bryant and Mrs. W. B. Hosmer.

These ladies, many of whom the Santa Maria Valley Historical Society had to research to recover their first names, are part of this book! These were married respectable ladies, proud of their husbands and determined to bring up the valley properly. They could see many problems ahead. Lost by an overwhelming majority was a motion to allow men to join. However, being respectable ladies, they concluded that for any serious matters, being of the gentler sex, they would consult their husbands for guidance.

By a week after the first meeting, twenty-eight new ladies were added to the membership. They all pledged themselves to an earnest study of good literature. The population of Santa Maria was close to 1,200 people.

Chapter Seven: Charitable Societies

In 1897 the ladies were focused on a having a park, complete with trees and flowers, where the community could gather for picnics and other important community events. For the development of Buena Vista Park, the ladies did consent to help from the husbands. Part of the plan included the digging of a well. This however failed, so the ladies carried water from their homes in their buggies to keep all of their hard work perky and lush. Buena Vista Park flourished under their attentive care. The park was turned over to the City of Santa Maria five months after the city's incorporation.

The club went through a name change in 1906 to the Minerva Library Club, and the focus shifted to obtaining a library. In October 1908 the cornerstone was laid, and in 1909 the first library was completed. The club also provided funding to encourage the building of a bandstand on the library grounds.

Today's Minerva Club includes men and continues to adhere to its original mission statement.

Improvement Club

Improvement Club in the July 1909 parade.
Source: Santa Maria Valley Historical Society collection.

Organized in the fall of 1906, this club was born just as the town was developing its personality. The women, sensing some unsavory aspects, were thrust into the formation of this club to keep the nature of the town on the straight and narrow. A few determined women were at its head as it sprang into being, and within a few weeks it had a membership of over 200 women.

As its leadership would describe, Santa Maria had been particularly blessed, but into all communities, large and small, creeps in an element of a less than desirable nature. This club was dedicated to the eradication of that undesirable element.

The club was also about assisting those in need. It assisted families in times of extreme stress. For a widowed woman, an injured or ill father unable to care for his family financially, or a family incapacitated by the needs of a sick child, the ladies would step in to fill the gap in whatever way was needed. No one was left alone.

Santa Maria was a small community, and secrets were hard to keep. The club stepped into a situation where they had to investigate a case of cruelty. The ladies saw to it that a 6-year-old boy was removed from his parents, put into a desirable home and protected from his parents by legal procedure.

Mrs. James Lowden was the first president, and Mrs. P.O. Tietzen was elected after her. When Mrs. Tietzen left Santa Maria to make her home in Berkeley, Mrs. Lowden resumed the presidency.

About 1910 it was decided to ask the cooperation of the gentlemen of Santa Maria. They accepted and were admitted as honorary members, thus making it possible for the club to provide help otherwise not to be made available by the ladies alone.

TBDL Club

TBDL Club pennants
Source: Santa Maria Valley Historical Society collection.

Hazel Tietzen
Source: Santa Maria Valley Historical Society collection.

This was a club created by local girls in 1908 on January 2nd. A party of four girls met at the home of Hazel Tietzen at 503 S. Broadway for the purpose of organizing a Leap Year Club. The girls couldn't agree on a name for their club but didn't let that stop them from organizing the group. The letters stand for "To Be Decided Later." The object of their club was "to have a social time among the girls." The girls agreed on a starting number of thirteen to invite for membership. Initial membership included: Hazel Tietzen, Alfa Jones, Laro Jones, Laura Kortner, Sadie Glines, Minerva Dana, Zilda Marriott, Gertrude Smith, Lucile Bryant, Teresa McDonald, Madge Klink, Cecilia Harris, Eva Glines, Bessie Goodwin, Nettie Smith and Edith Adams. The girls were aged 15 to 22. Hazel, the lead organizer, was 17-years-old. The first order of business would be a Leap Year Dance to be held at the Golden Bear Hall on the 18th of January. The "Bears" were a group of young men, similar to the TBDL Club, who had a clubhouse in the 100 block of North Lincoln Street. The second meeting was held at Zilda Marriott's. At this meeting, program and punch committees were

Golden Bears Club (back left-to-right): Landon Bagby, Elwood Bryant, Emmett Trott, Fred Haslam, Archie Cline, Elmer Boyd, Dick Doane, Bert Smith; (front left-to-right): Bert Jessee, Lee Brown, Nelson Jones, Mac Langlois.
Source: Santa Maria Valley Historical Society collection.

established. It was also decided that each girl should invite a boy to the dance. The third meeting

Chapter Seven: Charitable Societies

was held at Lucile Bryant's home. After the committee reports, invitations to the dance were written. Gertrude Smith and Madge Klink each volunteered to sing solo between dances. The fifth meeting was about setting up a Valentine's dance. There was no after-action report discussed in the minutes on the first dance, but presumably it was a big success as they almost immediately planned the next occasion to mix with the boys. The location would be Hart's Hall, and each girl would bring a basket lunch for two. The baskets would be hidden, and a string attached for the boys to follow. Each basket would be numbered. The girls wearing a blindfold would pin an arrow on a heart to choose their supper partner.

While no reporting on the parties appear in meeting notes, another party always ensued. In March of 1908, a Saint Patrick's party was planned for girls only at McMillan's Hall to carry out a "masked high jinx." Of course, all of the girls also attended the Saint Patrick's dance held on the 24th at Richard's Hall.

The girls continued to meet regularly for years. They held events or social activities every month and then also attended dances and parties hosted by other organizations. The young women of the Santa Maria Valley had very active social lives. Even as marriage and adulthood overtook them, they had a most wonderful time growing up Santa Maria Valley style.

A to Z Club

Members of the A to Z Club
Source: Santa Maria Valley Historical Society collection.

A club devoted to "charitable endeavors on behalf of the needy" was formed February 16, 1920, at Hart's Hall. The club was named for its members just as in the Second World War, the 82nd Airborne earned its patch of two As and the title All American with its reputation of representing every state in the union. The charter membership of the club started, alphabetically, with Bessie, Dorothy, Irma and Winnie Adam and ended with Olympia and Daisy Zanetti, thus A to Z. The ladies in the middle included: Stella Smythe, Mildred Kelley, Pauline Martin, Mabel Blosser, Rowena Senich, Juanita Dana, Anna Mae Breen, Lizzie Gillespie, Belle Gillespie, Gladys Whitt, Fern Felts, Margaret Steele, Marjorie Kennedy, Francis Loomis, Litti Paulding and Gladys Froom. The club would continue throughout the Second World War. During that time, it took part in service-connected activities, including Ground Observer Corps and USO Canteen work.

Chapter Eight: The Stories They Tell

Some of us grow up on stories of our families, have grandparents or even great grandparents who give us at least a snapshot of their lives, loves and the ones before them. The oral history of our families is full of colorful, if slightly embellished, tales with larger-than-life examples of how they overcame, persevered and prevailed. It's hard not to think of these storytellers as just old people regaling us with past adventures seen through rose-colored glasses or in some instances very gloomy ones. Gaining perspective on the social backdrop of a period sometimes gives a new perspective to the emotional events that past generations lived: how and why they spoke the way they did and why they can't, even today, let go of that last bite in a Tupperware.

Out of the house, office ladies from the Union Sugar plant in Betteravia.
Source: Santa Maria Valley Historical Society collection.

There is so much enthusiasm today in our individual DNA. Kits make DNA publicly available and affordable to a great many people. The average person barely understands the reference in the name *23 and me*, but most certainly purchase it, not only to trace blood relationships but to speculate on probable genetic activity that is going on in their bodies at this very moment! Ancestry.com has become a giant in the industry helping subscribers with building family trees, connecting lost family lines and even establishing DNA links that solve decades-old crimes. We've only just cracked the code, but we can still barely use it.

What do historical societies, newspapers, and cemeteries provide with all of this technology at our fingertips? They provide documented verification and pictures. To hold an actual artifact still makes the link to our heritage more exciting. Confirming online that your "great-great" was part of the American Civil War is thrilling; seeing his military tunic appear out of mothballs from an old box in the attic is a totally different high. There's knowing and then there's seeing with your own eyes! History wasn't made virtually or lived online. Death was real, and most people witnessed it first hand; it wasn't pixelated. Growing up was a messy business.

Our ancestors did not start out equal and did not enjoy equal opportunity. Most of us are the most impressed by the ones who had the least and yet led our families to where we are today. Some of the Ladies of the Valley had better starting points or better opportunities through work or just sheer luck. Nancy Kelsey certainly encountered a series of unfortunate events, but in her own words, she was well satisfied with her life. She absolutely had no formal education and died dirt poor. One could argue that an advanced education for Ida Blochman set her up to have an easy life, but her child was murdered and the mystery never solved during her lifetime. How does one define an easy life? All of our ladies had challenges. What made each of them outstanding was how they rose to those challenges. Whether they had an arranged marriage, a love match, wealth or hardship, they all made a lasting impression and left an amazing legacy for all of us. They built us a community.

Dedications

Thank you to everyone who contributed to the Santa Maria Valley Historical Society's effort to publish the first edition of the ladies' book.

The next few ladies have been added by members and friends of the historical society who wanted to recognize a special woman that helped inform their life. We hope you will enjoy these additional heroines.

Inga Elizabeth Jensen Nielsen (1905-1988)

Inga was born in Nipomo and became a resident of Santa Maria in 1925. She moved to Santa Maria after her marriage to C.C. Marinus Nielson, originally of Denmark. Inga was a homemaker who acquired several skills and talents throughout her life. She was a Red Cross volunteer during World War II, a lifetime member of St. Peter's Episcopal Church, Minerva Club, Order of the Eastern Star, Danish Ladies Society and the Santa Maria Valley Historical Society.

As part of the Historical Society, Inga buried a note in a time capsule for her grandson David Nielsen who was able to attend the capsule opening and receive the letter written years before by her for him.

An avid gardener, Inga filled her world with beautiful flowers and fruit trees. Friends continue to be welcome to visit and enjoy her garden as it continues to thrive at Rancho El Caelca.

Inga was mother to Pauline (Taylor) and Carl Nielsen, grandmother of seven (Steven, Jeanne, Jeanette, Teri, Christopher, Sara and David) and great-grandmother of six (Josh, Nathan, Matthew, Kristen, Taylor, Rudy and Samson.)

Viola Onorina (Rena) Rollini Perry (1928-2016)

Rena grew up on her parent's dairy farm. She graduated from Santa Maria High School in 1946. She was an active Campfire Girls leader, a member of the Miller Street Mother's Club and a founding partner, with her husband, of Perry's Electric Motors & Control. She was also a dedicated fruit and vegetable gardener. She and her daughter, Virginia Souza, founded a non-profit entity which became the Santa Maria Natural History Museum.

Dedications

Marian Svensrud Acquistapace (1907-1983)

Marian was born in North Dakota to Anton and Mary Svensrud. She arrived in the Santa Maria Valley in 1932 as an educator. She taught for seven years at Santa Maria High School. She also taught in the Santa Maria Elementary School District before she retired. She was a member of the Minerva Club and the American Association of University Women. Marian was married to Leo Acquistapace, who was a lifelong resident of the valley. Together they had three sons: Leo, Jim and Bobby. Marian's experiences lead her to serve on many boards including Allan Hancock College. She was a founding member of the Santa Maria Valley Historical Society.

Ethel M. Neiggemann (1909-2001)

Ethel was born in Streator, Illinois. She came to Santa Maria in 1939 with her husband Henry, who worked as an engineer assisting in building Sisters Hospital. Primarily a homemaker, she also worked for several years as a clerk in Mae Moore and Peggy's Fashions in old downtown Santa Maria. She was known and remembered as a giving person with an indomitable spirit. Born with only one hand, she accomplished everything life presented to her with great enthusiasm. She often demonstrated to skeptical acquaintances how she tied her shoelaces. She delighted her grandchildren by playing songs of the 20s and 30s on the piano. She attended First Christian Church. She was an inspiration to her children Catherine Rudolph, Marita Green, Michael Neiggemann and stepson Hank Neiggemann. Ethel had 11 grandchildren and 15 great-grandchildren.

Dedications

Elsie Margaret Patterson Bumann (1914-1986)

Elsie was from a native of Los Alamos, California, family. She was the great-granddaughter of Benjamin Foxen and Eduarda Osuna. Born in Santa Maria, she graduated from Santa Maria High School in 1932. She was an outstanding student having graduated from the Queen of Angels School of Nursing with the highest test score in California. She served at County Hospital, Sisters Hospital and finally as first charge nurse in the emergency room at Marian Hospital. She was a registered nurse for more than 27 years and the first person people in Los Alamos went to for medical emergencies. Elsie was a co-founder of the Los Alamos Just-a-Mere Club, an "Old Days" Grand Marshall, a member and past president of the Los Alamos Senior Citizens and actively involved with Meals-On-Wheels, delivering hot lunches to those in need. She was also a member of the Santa Maria Valley Historical Society. Else was a fourth-generation Foxen; the seventh generation still lives on Foxen property in Los Alamos.

These ladies and the others in this book have been carefully researched, but it is difficult to catch their amazing strengths of perseverance, their dedication to community, the absolute power and fortitude these women brought to building and shaping our Santa Maria Valley.

www.ingramcontent.com/pod-product-compliance
Lightning Source LLC
Chambersburg PA
CBHW080613230426
43664CB00019B/2882